The Portfolio as a Learning Strategy

The cover of a book is a great way to introduce the content and purpose of it. In this case the title alone indicates the intention of the authors. Working from the title, I incorporated different symbols and pictures to express its meaning. Having done a portfolio myself, I understand the purpose and benefit behind this learning strategy. I interpret the portfolio as a method of learning that helps students keep track of their progress. It also helps students understand what level they started at and how they progressed. In addition, the portfolio focuses on their goals for growth and improvement. Students learn from this process because they determine their progress by looking at a collection of their own works. They can visually see how they have progressed and how they can further improve. From my experiences with this process, several words come to mind when I think of a portfolio. A portfolio means progress and advancement in the level and quality of work. That is why I have included footprints, keys, and a wheel. A portfolio also means building; this is represented by the bricks that form the title. Students use their first work as a foundation for improvement and as a basis for their skills. The light bulb shows that a learning strategy like this provides room for new ideas and creativity along with learning. Most importantly, I have included the globe because this is a method that can be used in different subjects and languages. All types of classes can monitor their progress with the portfolio. If the portfolio were to be described in one word, I would call it progress.

Tiffany Khun Hor, Grade 12
reflection on cover drawing

The PORTFOLIO as a LEARNING STRATEGY

Carol Porter
Janell Cleland

Boynton/Cook Publishers
HEINEMANN
Portsmouth, NH

Boynton/Cook Publishers, Inc.
A subsidiary of Reed Elsevier Inc.
361 Hanover Street
Portsmouth, NH 03801
Offices and agents throughout the world

Editor: Dawn Boyer
Production: J. B. Tranchemontagne
Cover and interior design: Mary Cronin
Cover illustration based on drawing by: Tiffany Khun Hor

Every effort has been made to contact the copyright holders for permission to reprint borrowed material where necessary. We regret any oversights that may have occurred and would be happy to rectify them in future printings of this work.

The authors and publisher wish to thank those who have generously given permission to reprint borrowed material:

Excerpts from "St. Francis Sister Creates Award-Winning Pie Crust" by Theresa Staley. Originally published in *The Observer* (Summer 1984). Reprinted by permission.

Excerpts from "A 'Blue Ribbon Nun'" by Sue Marcotte. Originally published in *Catholic Post* (Summer 1984). Reprinted by permission.

Book cover from *Blind Date* by R.L. Stine. Jacket illustration copyright © 1987 by Scholastic Inc. Reprinted by permission.

Book cover from *Mindbend* by Robin Cook. Copyright © 1985 by Robin Cook. Used by permission of Dutton Signet, a division of Penguin Books USA Inc.

Book cover from *Mortal Fear* by Robin Cook. Copyright © 1988 by Robin Cook. Reprinted by permission of The Putnam Berkeley Group.

Library of Congress Cataloging-in-Publication Data

Porter, Carol (Carol J.)
    The portfolio as a learning strategy / Carol Porter, Janell
        Cleland. p. cm.
        Includes bibliographical references and index.
        ISBN 0–86709–348–X
    1. Portfolios in education.   I. Cleland, Janell.   II. Title.
LB1029.P67P65 1995
371.3—dc20   94–3522
                                                     CIP

Printed in the United States of America on acid-free paper.
99 98 97 96 95   EB   1 2 3 4 5 6 7 8 9

*Dedicated to
our families, colleagues, and students
who have and continue to
support and inspire our learning.*

Contents

Foreword

As I read *The Portfolio As A Learning Strategy*, by Carol Porter and Janell Cleland, I kept recalling my first encounter with these two outstanding teachers, whom I have seen a number of times since our first meeting. I was at a whole language conference in the Chicago area about three years ago and was interested in their workshop. I wanted to see how high-school teachers use portfolios. Since I am often questioned about the role of whole language in secondary schools, I thought I'd gain general insights as well. I remember the large auditorium-like room, because I was greeted with students' work displayed on the walls and on the table in front of the speaker. The room was crowded with teachers eager to consider the use of portfolios. Carol and Janell[1] kept their audience's interest throughout. It was obvious that the presenters were experienced junior-high and high-school teachers.

I was impressed with Janell and Carol's enthusiasm about the role of portfolios in their classes. More importantly, I sensed their strong belief in the learning abilities and potentials of their students. Initially, the focus of their concerns were those students who needed the greatest support to be successful in secondary schools. However, they soon discovered that portfolios could enhance the learning of all students as well as themselves as teachers.

Now, through this publication, their journey of inquiry into portfolio use over a number of years is documented to help elementary, and secondary and college or university teachers looking for similar alternatives. To talk about portfolios, the authors tell their story through constant self-reflection. They wrestle with their personal and collective struggles to develop the best ways for portfolios to serve their students, enhance their teaching, and share with other professionals. The presentation of their practices is documented within the context of daily school life and reflects the important relationships that Carol and Janell discovered exist between theory and practice, curriculum and instruction, self-assessment, and continuous planning within a collaborative community. Through their in-depth self-reflection, Carol and Janell have come to understand the significance of portfolios as a learning strategy for all learners, regardless of age.

This use of portfolios embodies a number of important concepts or principles for teachers concerned with learning process, with whole language teaching, or with involving students in serious self-reflection of their own learning and their own work. One important principle is that evaluation tools are most useful when they continue over time, when they involve the students in decision making about what and how to evaluate, and when they inform the ongoing curriculum. Carol and Janell provide many examples of such influences from their uses of portfolios.

---

[1] I consciously use first names in this foreword. It represents my friendship with the authors, follows their pattern of the use of their first names, and establishes a style of informality.

Building on John Dewey's ideas, they establish clearly that learning results from "doing" by both teachers and students. The authors set the stage by saying to their audience, "Find a place to start, even if you make a mistake." Through my own work with pre-service and in-service teachers, I am aware that it is never enough to read books about doing research or putting curriculum innovations into practice. It is only when teachers/researchers become immersed in their inquiry or teaching experiences that their reading, conversation, and self-reflection take on meaning.

The mistakes teachers/researchers make when they are actively involved in using or exploring the use of portfolios, for example, provide the opportunities to examine processes closely and to consider carefully how to proceed. Learning does not proceed without mistakes. The authors share their errors (miscues) and the importance of rethinking and reflecting on their wrong turns as they journey toward the development of more effective teaching and evaluation strategies.

By learning from their mistakes, which I prefer to call miscues, professionals have many opportunities to change and adapt inappropriate practices, especially when they respond to their students' learning. Because of the importance of these dynamics, I strongly urge that administrators avoid turning portfolio use into formulaic, standardized routines through district mandates. Many successful instructional activities taking place in whole language and innovative classrooms are becoming institutionalized and routinized. Mandates are harmful to the process of teachers taking responsibility for making informed decisions. Perhaps it is important to explain why.

Innovative practices, such as portfolios, are developed from theoretical beliefs, knowledge, and principles that include establishing alternatives to standardized measures; providing opportunities for choice; encouraging change; and using evaluation as a source for curriculum building and understanding students. Significant innovation and change come from constant attention to the impact of such tools on students' learning, on parents' understandings, and on the development of a rich, exciting curriculum

It is unfortunate when people who have different beliefs and understandings co-opt instructional events without understanding the theory that informs those particular practices. Since they are unaware of the theoretical issues that support the use of portfolios, in this instance, professionals with differing points of view apply their own belief systems that demand standardization, grades, and prepackaged materials. As a result, innovative practice becomes an institutionalized routine. It's never the same after that. The excitement and power of portfolios come from teachers such as Janell and Carol who have invented the uses of portfolios with their students. This book provides a road map for other knowledgeable and interested teachers to adapt to their terrain. It is not to be followed slavishly, but needs to be used as a demonstration of possibilities.

This book is written for all teachers at every level of the school continuum. Those who teach college and university students should attend carefully to the lessons Carol and Janell have learned. I'm working on developing ideas for the use of portfolios with pre-service and in-service teachers with my colleagues. The ideas from the authors will help introduce into college courses the principles, ideas, and instructional practices that are necessary to challenge the rigidity of most of tertiary education. We must find ways to practice what we preach, especially in teacher-education programs. The work of Janell and Carol can move us in this direction.

Janell and Carol document the ways in which they answered their questions as they were developing the use of portfolios with their students. They share the books they read, the conferences that influenced them, the discussions they had with each other and their students, and the responses of parents, administrators, and teachers. This inquiry process in which the authors engaged highlights and exemplifies the role of teachers/researchers in educational institutions. The authors provide their readers with powerful profiles or language stories reflecting their students' anxieties, disappointments, and growth. They discuss the lessons that they learn from these stories, showing how they are learners at the same time that they are teachers/researchers. Such is the nature of reflective teaching. They are researchers because they are asking questions significant to their own learning. They say on page 152, "We have found questions to be our strategy for extending knowledge, not a convenient obstacle for standing still."

Related to the teacher/researcher issue is the way in which Carol and Janell show that raising what they do to a conscious level informs their practice. The portfolio allows this consciousness-raising to be available not only to the audience of this book, not only to inform their teaching, but most importantly to their students. For too long, what we do in school has been mystifying for many students. They don't know why they are writing or reading what is assigned. Such students let school happen to them through school days, months, and years, but do not become engaged in their own learning. Carol and Janell show how portfolios as a learning strategy help students demystify reading and writing. Learning in school does not remain a series of instructional activities to be done for a grade or to please parents or teachers. It is a powerful experience that students come to understand is significant to them and can impact their lives both inside and outside of school. Understanding the ways in which Carol and Janell use portfolios demystifies learning for students. As a result, students also become self-reflective and involved in inquiring into their own learning.

This is not just a book about portfolios. It is a research narrative about two professional teachers examining their own teaching and learning to enhance their teaching practices by highlighting and understanding the successes and failures of their students' learning. At the same time, their narrative provides a wealth of information so other teachers benefit from their experiences.

Yetta M. Goodman

Kristin age 7.

WHEN WE AGREED to co-author this book, many questions surfaced. One of the most pressing was, "How do you write a book?" It was only a few years ago that we began sharing our writing with students. Since then, essays, reflections, and journal entries have become part of our daily life; but a *book*? We soon realized, of course, that this was a question for which there was no canned, packaged, or right answer. The uncertainty, apprehension, and confusion that we experienced were not all that different from the feelings we had when we first tried portfolios in our classrooms. We had wanted someone to tell us what procedures to follow then, too. With the book, we wanted the words we chose to be right, just as we wanted our presentation of portfolios to our students to be right. We also knew that we would make many mistakes along the way. Advice we often give to our students and to teachers who feel discomfort about beginning to write or initiate portfolios was advice we needed to give ourselves: Find a place to start, even if you make a few mistakes.

We discovered that our starting place was also the beginning of the revision process, both of our writing and of understanding about the potential of portfolios. Even in our mistakes, we found a few nuggets that we could save and take with us to second draft. We hope that, as teachers begin experimenting with their first drafts of portfolio implementation, they, too, can find a few nuggets worth saving to take with them into their second effort. Our learning story is both a shared and individual personal narrative. We hope that you, the reader, understand that the use of "we" and "our" represents our shared story while the words Carol and Janell are used when individual stories are being told. To have used any other style of writing would have negated the collaborative relationship we have shared in our classrooms, our learning, and our writing.

Asking questions and seeking the answers together had been the basis of our working relationship since the fall of 1989. We were both hired to teach at Mundelein High School (MHS) during the summer of 1987. Janell moved to the Chicago area so her husband could attend graduate school; Carol had taught middle school for thirteen years and was looking for a position as a reading teacher. Janell was hired to teach three speech classes and two freshman English classes. Carol was assigned five remedial reading classes.

Even though our teaching assignments were similar, our teaching paths never crossed because Janell was a member of the English/Social Studies Division, and Carol's division was titled Reading/Media Center. Each division within the school was led by a divisional supervisor whose role was similar to that of a department chairperson. As new teachers seem to do, we sought each other out if we had the same lunch period and sat together at all-school functions. However, very seldom did talk turn to curriculum, instruction, or assessment.

Midway through our second year at Mundelein, Carol's divisional supervisor, who was teaching a Chapter I class, expressed concern about the "supervised study hall" format offered to students in the Chapter I classes. She asked Carol to help her revise the course and write a grant application, hoping to transform it into a writing lab. Carol was also teaching several Chapter I classes that year and agreed that the program resembled a bandage over an at-risk student's problem, merely focusing on getting the student through school on a day-to-day basis. As Carol and her supervisor began to plan, Carol expressed concern about creating a course focused only on writing without also teaching reading.

It is possible that Janell was brought into the Chapter I Reading/Writing Lab discussion at this point because she was the person with writing expertise and Carol was the reading expert. In reality, we think that both divisional supervisors had been pushing for a writing lab for several years, and this was a way for them to get a part of what they wanted without losing all of the Chapter I funding to the other division. A day or two after the idea of a Reading/Writing Lab emerged, we met with both divisional supervisors. They thought our first step should include visiting neighboring school districts to examine their writing labs and look for suggestions and ideas about how ours should be set up.

Since there was a climate of distrust among the members of each division about subject areas and teaching styles, it was with great caution that we began to talk about possible teaching assignments. We found we had one thing in common and got a sense that our teaching partnership was off to a positive start when Janell asked Carol "Which schools should we visit?" Carol responded that she didn't want to visit any other schools because ours was unique to any around us, which was the response Janell had hoped for.

Mundelein is located forty-five miles northwest of Chicago. Most of the surrounding school districts have enrollments that are nearly double the twelve-hundred students at MHS. The socioeconomic status of most of those families in neighboring districts is also twice that of students at Mundelein High. Over the past six years, Mundelein has experienced an increase in the number of minority students in what has historically been a blue-collar community. Our Latino population composes 20 percent of our student body, with 4 percent Asian population and 2 percent African American. Although the number of low-income families and mobility rates are not as high as state percentages, they are high in comparison to most schools in our county. The number of limited-English-proficient students in our school is greater than the state average. These factors made it impossible for us to fund the types of programs neighboring school districts provided for their students. Even if this were not true, we believed the needs of our students were different from the needs of student populations elsewhere.

In the weeks before summer break (we will now admit to each other), we found ourselves walking slowly past each other's classroom to catch a glimpse of what was going on. As we became braver, each of us found reasons to step through the doorway to deliver a message to a student or each other. We saw that many aspects of our teaching were similar. We had to search to find the teacher since she was not in front of the room lecturing, but was sitting among the students reading, writing, and discussing. The bulletin boards and walls were covered with student work.

What we were seeing in each other's classroom was certainly not what we had expected or were led to believe. It was probably this contradiction between expectation and reality that led us to be honest about our apprehensions and beliefs as we began to talk about the needs of the teenagers who were soon to be our students.

We discovered that we were both anxious to service the students who generally "fell through the cracks": students who no longer qualified for the bilingual program but, because of their language deficiency, were placed in low-track classes; students placed in lower-track classes as early as first grade and had continued with that label permanently attached; and students who sat in their average-track classes mechanically going through the motions of being a student; or students who were putting forth immense effort only to earn C's and D's.

Most of the students who would be sitting in our classrooms believed that reading and writing were difficult for them because they didn't try hard enough. Many thought that if they would just slow down, read "harder," or recopy that piece of writing more neatly, then they would be more successful. Most of our students had been told this for most of their educational career, and they were perfectly willing to accept any blame for their perceived deficiencies. We agreed that we wanted to arm them with a variety of strategies that they could rely on whenever they needed to make sense of what they read or whenever they needed to revise a piece of writing. Most of all, we wanted our students to experience the sense of joy that can accompany completing a novel after staying up all night reading because you just couldn't put it down. We wanted them to know that sense of pride that wells up when someone asks to read something you wrote because they heard it was great.

Perhaps our vision was a bit simplistic, but we decided that, with the population of students we had targeted for the Reading/Writing Lab, we wanted to do exactly the opposite of what they had experienced instructionally in the past. We reasoned that, "if the same methods had been used for ten to twelve years and they hadn't worked, wasn't it time to try something else?" Since we knew that the reading materials our low-track students had grown up with were short stories and worksheets, we decided that the students should be reading novels and writing about their reading. Since most of these students wrote only occasionally and most often on essay exams, we thought that they should choose the formats and topics for their writing. Whenever students weren't reading, they should be writing or discussing with other learners as a way to revise their ideas.

As we look back on the plan we presented to our divisional supervisors, we are surprised that they agreed – risk-taking was not valued by the administration. In fact, the academic climate strongly discouraged nontraditional teaching methods and maintained they should be avoided. We think the course label of "lab" and the fact that our idea had much more structure to it than the writing centers other school districts had in place were, perhaps, reasons that we were allowed to move forward with our plans.

Frequent meetings over the summer confirmed what we had begun to suspect and fueled our excitement about working together: We had similar philosophies about learning. We knew that learners learn by doing and our individual classrooms reflected that belief. Students learned to read and write in our classrooms by listening to each other's ideas, by taking risks with words and sentences, and by experimenting with reading and writing in ways that they could use when they left our classrooms.

Neither of us believed that we could tell our students how to read, to write, or to speak. Each of us had experienced teachers who tried to tell us, when we were students, how to do these things. We knew we really didn't learn until we determined what worked for us. Trying to find real-life examples of our philosophy, we knew that people can be told how to ride a bicycle, roll out a pie crust, drive a car, use a word processor, or shoot a basketball. Simply acquiring the knowledge from a source does not provide the ability to internalize the learning. You learn by doing. We were anxious to provide an environment for our students that gave them the opportunity to learn *in* our classroom the same way they learn *outside* the classroom.

At that time, the professional literature we were reading suggested that educators organize curriculum around a theme, genre, or author study. Even though these professional books were intended for elementary classrooms (and the majority of those published still are), we thought that we should be able to apply this idea to the secondary classroom. After all, we reasoned, how we learn shouldn't change as we get older. It's what we learn that changes. So, we thought the thematic structure should work as long as the themes were supported with materials that were appropriate for secondary students.

When we talked about how we would bring together the Reading/Writing Lab students in their new educational community, we considered the situation we had been placed in just a few months before by our divisional supervisors. We realized that we hadn't become productive in our planning and learning until we had gotten to know each other. So our own recent personal experiences, in tandem with our past efforts to have students share their ideas and work with one another, led us to search for a way to begin the first weeks of our new classes.

We decided to begin the school year with the strategy *Getting to Know You* (Harste, Short, and Burke 1988, 274-276), which involves partners interviewing each other, preparing a written rough draft as an introduction, sharing the rough draft with the class to gain ideas, revising, editing, and publishing. Although the real community is built when rough drafts are shared (authors' circle), we celebrated our new family by taking pictures of all the students and displayed these on a bulletin board alongside final drafts. Later, these went into a class book when new pieces of writing were published. *Getting to Know You* also modeled a curricular and instructional framework called the "authoring cycle" (Harste, Short, and Burke 1988) with which Carol had experimented at the middle school, so this strategy served as an excellent introduction to the way in which we would approach learning in our classrooms.

Since we wanted to keep our newly created community intact and we knew we were facing many reluctant readers, we agonized over the choice of novels that our students would read first. We had already worked with many of the students who had enrolled in the Reading/Writing Lab, so we knew the resistance and reluctance with which they would approach a novel. We wanted a book that would grab the students' attention right away and hold it enough that they would forget that they were engaged in what they traditionally viewed with disdain. Carol recommended the book *Crazy Horse Electric Game* by Chris Crutcher because a student in one of her reading classes risked missing his varsity baseball game since he had stayed up most of the night reading it and then overslept. Janell took it home to read and called Carol the next day to say she thought it would accomplish the purpose. After that first novel, we wanted students to be able to choose novels that they wanted to read, so we began to gather novels and set up interest centers that related in some way to the themes, characters, and conflicts in *Crazy Horse Electric Game*.

We realized that we were going to be implementing some dramatic instructional changes. We decided that the students needed to see how serious we were about the changes from the minute they entered their new learning environment: Each of our classrooms had to look different from the traditional classrooms in which students had previously enrolled. We set the desks in circles and established interest centers that corresponded to the various themes found in the novel. There was one bulletin board for student work, another for newspaper articles pertaining to our school and students, and another that invited everyone to share their areas of expertise so students could consult each other throughout the school year. One table was filled with all the writing supplies we could acquire: crayons, markers, colored pencils, colored paper, construction paper, graph paper, stickers, scissors, tape, etc. Tape recorders were available as were tapes with the songs mentioned in the first novel we were reading. Six Apple® II E computers lined the wall and every student had a personal disk ready to be filled. A high-school version of the "cubby" or mailbox was established, and students checked their folders daily for correspondence from us and each other. A fish tank appeared later in the school year, and one student evolved as our resident fish expert. We kept a log at the side of the tank, and students recorded their thoughts and reactions as they watched the fish. There was a newspaper and magazine center, and any empty space that was left was filled with novels that begged students to open them to see if this one was right for them.

As the semester progressed, no day was "typical." Some examples of what you might see if you visited our classrooms included the sharing of our reactions to the previous night's reading by referring to comments we had written on our bookmarks (see chapter 4); an authors' circle to share a piece of writing; students at computers revising their writing; students reading; and other students conferencing with us. The class might be analyzing a series of bookmarks to set reading goals for the remaining chapters in a novel, or they might be reflecting on how well they met their goals if they had completed the novel. It is also possible that everyone may be busy reading or writing while we take the time to jot down anecdotal records that Yetta Goodman (1989) refers to as "kidwatching."

The days passed quickly during our first semester together, and the success stories were more dramatic than any we had previously experienced. The issue of grading, however, plagued us at the end of each six-weeks grading period. We wholeheartedly agreed with Harman when she said "tests offer a limited choice of superficial answers, one and only one of which can be right . . . Therefore, the curriculum must also consist of facts and details rather than personalized, open-ended inquiry . . . This test-like curriculum denies teachers the opportunity to behave like professionals—to exercise discretion, ingenuity, creativity, and independence" (1989-1990, 7). Traditional assessment procedures simply did not meet the needs of our students. How could we incorporate the reading and writing goals that students so thoughtfully set and worked so hard to achieve? How could we document a senior boy's excitement over finishing the first novel in his high school career? And how could we label the piece of writing that one girl nervously shared about how she continues to agonize over her adoption? With the required semester exams only a few weeks away, we began to search for alternatives. Our concerns were further fueled by Yetta Goodman's article "Evaluation in Whole Language Classrooms" (1989). She maintained that there were five important issues to consider in regard to evaluation: (a) evaluation is continuous and cumulative (b) evaluation is interpretive (c) evaluation involves self-evaluation for both the teacher and the learners (d) evaluation takes many forms (e) evaluation informs curriculum and at the same time is informed by curriculum. In the same article she mentions the use of portfolios to evaluate oral language, reading, writing, and concept development. Maybe this was the answer to our assessment dilemma. We decided to try portfolios within our classrooms.

Although Goodman's article provided a theoretical basis for our decisions, articles on the actual use of portfolios within the classroom were not available prior to our first attempt to incorporate them in our curriculum. As a result, we generated a list of questions about portfolio use. What should go into a portfolio? How can we incorporate the issues Goodman had challenged us to consider? If the portfolio can support learning, how will the students make sense of the materials they put into their portfolios? How can the portfolio be put together? What should we do with the completed portfolio?

Next we determined our best answers to these questions and proceeded into final exam week. We decided that our primary objective was for students to return to their work from the previous semester and analyze their changes as readers and writers. Many of our decisions had a political basis, however. Our classes had transformed into something so dramatically different from other English and reading classrooms in the building, that other teachers began to suspect we coddled students and lowered the high standards of achievement for English and reading classes. Since we were hearing these types of accusatory comments and had deviated so much from traditional materials and instruction, we were cautious about going too far out on the limb with our assessment instruments. What we really wanted to do with our assessment instrument and, politically speaking, what we felt we needed to do, required a compromise. That compromise resulted in the use of teacher-directed portfolios.

We told the students to put into their portfolios their first through final drafts of all pieces of writing they had completed. We also asked the students to display their journal entries or other responses for each novel read during the semester. Finally, we prepared a series of questions about each draft of writing and about the responses to literature from each book that was read (see chapter 3) for the students to answer.

At the end of exam week, we found ourselves sitting side by side at our desks surrounded by those first portfolios, wondering exactly what we had gotten ourselves into. As we read through our students' reflections, it became apparent that we had been too directive, not only about the items that should go into the portfolio, but also about what should be said about each item. Many answers directed us to reread previous answers or expressed an angry tone beginning with "As I said before . . . ." We realized that our directiveness had not only forced students to take the easy way out in terms of thoughtful responses, but we had also kept the students from digging below the surface to discover the changes that had taken place in their literacy development. Looking back at this portfolio version of a final exam, we felt great about our growth as teachers, but at the same time we felt awful. It was reminiscent of the accomplishment of making it around the block on a bicycle for the first time, yet aching from the scrapes and bruises covering both hands and knees. Those little wounds and scars reminded us that we still had much to learn and many questions to be answered.

Throughout second semester we continued to search for literature on portfolios and came away empty-handed. Then we turned to journals written for artists, thinking that professionals in that field might have suggestions that we could transfer to portfolio use in the classroom. Sheila Watts stated "A truly successful portfolio will reveal the way artists think, because an important part of any illustration assignment is the way they solve the problem at hand" (1990, 74). This gave us a starting point for discussion and planning. What if the students in our classes used the portfolio to display the way they think and how they solve the problems they encounter as learners? From this perspective we could also imagine that just as one artist viewing another artist's portfolio might gain insight into his or her own approaches to learning, so too could the learner who read another learner's portfolio. The idea that the author of the portfolio is not the only one who learns gave us a starting point from which to revise our ideas about portfolios.

Our investigation also took us to articles on authentic assessment; we were most challenged by the ideas of Wiggins as we searched for the "authentic" test that reflected the four basic characteristics he discussed. He says that the authentic test should be performance-based and place a greater focus on teaching and learning the criteria to be used in the assessment (1989). There should be an increased awareness of self-assessment as students present and defend themselves publicly to ensure genuine mastery. At this point in our development, we still saw portfolios as our "authentic" alternative to testing and most of the publications we could find viewed them in this light, but we were not entirely comfortable with this narrow view of portfolios.

When second-semester exams approached, we were ready to try this whole business of portfolios again. This time we were more honest with our students. We introduced the concept of portfolios as an assessment tool that could mirror the thinking process of each person. Beyond assessment we weren't sure about their potential, which was the reason we needed their ideas, help, and suggestions. As we began to value student voice in assessment the way we had in the learning experiences throughout the semester, we discovered that exciting learning experiences occurred as students spread their folders over desks, tables, and the floor to rediscover bits and pieces of their previous encounters with reading, writing, and learning.

We had support and encouragement from our divisional supervisors during that first year and we believe that our pro-active stance as we embarked on research created the type of relationship with our supervisors that most teachers wish they could have. In her second year at Mundelein High School (the year prior to the creation of the Reading/Writing Lab), Carol, along with her supervisor, set a teaching goal to read professional literature, try new strategies in her classroom, and report her findings. Each month Carol provided her supervisor with copies of articles that had influenced her instructional decisions and a narrative that described her resulting classroom experiences. The shared articles and reflections later became the focal point of discussions with her supervisor. Together, Carol and her supervisor determined how she might alter instruction. The supervisor then provided feedback from classroom observations that gave data from which to draw conclusions and plan future investigations. In the year that Carol and Janell began working together, Carol chose alternative assessment as a topic to research. In retrospect, Carol sees that without knowing it, she laid the ground work for her inquiry and was given support primarily because her supervisor was learning along with her through the research, literature, and discussions that Carol provided.

We used similar approaches to gain support and encouragement for our students and the program with parents. Keeping them informed about what we were doing and why we were doing it through correspondence and conferences was crucial to the implementation of an alternative assessment instrument. During the second semester, since we had involved our students in researching and learning about portfolios, they were actually our best advocates for change. The students could discuss with their parents how they were beginning to understand their learning process, and, as a result, they understood how their assessment needs were also changing.

Our students' interest fueled our enthusiasm, and we began to actively solve the problems we encountered with traditional assessment by approaching our learning as researchers. This was a dramatic change for two classroom teachers who once thought that research was reserved only for scientists in a laboratory or professors in an ivory tower at some university. Thankfully those mythical ivory-tower people set us straight. Perhaps the most memorable experience that shattered the ivory-tower myth came the day Yetta Goodman attended our session on portfolios at a Chicago area conference. She viewed us as classroom researchers.

A big change occurred once we began to view ourselves as researchers; we allowed ourselves to accept our mistakes. For us, this was a much altered view of ourselves as professionals. Our old notion was that, as classroom teachers, we had to have all the right answers in order to maintain our authority with the students, and we couldn't afford to make any mistakes because we were in charge of our students' learning. Ironically, this meant that we were working under two sets of rules for learning: one set that we forced ourselves to live by and another set that we allowed students to live by. Why is it that we, like most teachers, could accept the fact that children learn from their mistakes, but we will not allow that flexibility in our own growth and development?

No one expects that the first utterances from a child's mouth will be grammatically correct any more than we expect that a youngster's first attempt to pitch a ball over home plate will be a strike. We accept approximations in our students because we know these are the points from which learning can grow. Admittedly, we owe it to our students to be as well-informed about portfolios prior to our approximations in the classroom, but eventually teachers as learners need to take the first step, knowing they, too, can learn from their mistakes. We believe the biggest mistakes we as teachers can make in terms of student learning is to stop ourselves from learning.

We have watched many teachers in what has now become the Communication Arts division, Teachers Applying Whole Language (TAWL) group, and at in-service workshops begin their implementation of portfolios from a different vantage point than we did. One teacher, who categorized himself as being very traditional, decided to incorporate reading strategies along with the reading of literature. He then used the portfolio as a way for students to explore how they had changed as readers and which strategies were the most successful for them. Another teacher created a theme unit with her students and implemented the portfolio as a reflective tool for student analysis of their process and the transformation of their understanding of that theme. Still another teacher decided to add the dimension of student choice to instruction in her classroom as students worked toward meeting their individual reading and writing goals. She no longer chose the novels or assigned the writing topics. The portfolios her students assembled focused on the choices they made and the degree to which they accomplished their goals. A portion of their reflective analysis considered how much the element of choice influenced the accomplishment of their reading and writing goals.

Realizing that we all have different concepts, needs, interests, experiences, and instructional histories and situations, we have chosen not to present our ideas in a "how to" manner. We hope that you will author ideas with us (Harste, Short, and Burke). Just as no two readers would have the same interpretations of a piece of literature, so too should there be a wide range of learning possibilities and interpretations for the use of portfolios. Like reading, writing, and speaking, portfolio implementation is a process. If we had been trying to accomplish everything we do now with portfolios in our first attempt three years ago, the task would have seemed insurmountable. We probably would have rationalized reasons for the failure of portfolios without ever trying them. We hope that educators can learn from our reflections on our learning process. Educators should feel satisfied with their development and the answers they have found, but also need to remember that learning begins and continues with inquiry. We still have questions; we feel we're not finished, but we're confident the portfolio as a learning strategy can support our future inquiry. At one time, the abstract nature of working toward perfection but never reaching it was unsettling for us as teachers. Today it stirs within us an excitement about what might lie beyond our current imaginations.

Just as we generated questions as we began using portfolios and writing this book, we continued to generate questions as the book progressed. We share our new questions with you at the end of each chapter, and we invite you to pose your own questions, formulate tentative answers, revise your ideas, and take those first steps to bring portfolios into your classroom so you can continue to learn by doing. We encourage you to listen to voices other than ours as you read a variety of materials on portfolios and discuss their potential with friends; however, we hope that by sharing our decision-making process our readers can begin to understand that early attempts with portfolios should not be considered mistakes but rather points of departure for moving beyond current understanding. "We love errors and invite you to love them too. Nothing should scare you more than groups or persons who think they know all the answers. Good learners always encounter errors that make them itch professionally" (Watson, Burke, and Harste 1989). The errors we made while exploring the use of portfolios with our students helped us to determine where we were as learners, how we arrived at that point, and where we needed to go next. We invite you to learn from our errors and encounter a few of your own as you experiment with portfolios as a strategy for learning.

BRYAN WAS KNOWN by his high school peers as the next Stephen King. Not only had he read all of King's books several times, but he also wrote stories that emulated King's writing style, which Bryan found so engaging. Bryan was equally well known throughout the English department as a student who displayed great talent *when* he chose to work and as a student whose choice of authors was too limited. Carol was Bryan's eighth-grade English teacher, and she had begun to have students choose their own topics for writing. She also used authors' circles to help students gain ideas for revision. Carol remembers that the whole class wanted to listen to Bryan's stories, and they sought him out to get feedback on their writing. She knew Bryan was a talented writer and, the week before graduation, she asked him to consider dedicating one of his books to her when he became famous.

A year later, Carol accepted a teaching position at Mundelein High School, across the street from her previous school but in a different school district. She saw Bryan occasionally in the hallway and, from time to time, he would share his latest piece of writing with her. Invariably, students would draw near and ask if they could read, too.

Carol was surprised when she saw Bryan walk through the door of her Chapter I classroom with an admit slip to enter the program. He had very little to say in response to Carol's questions concerning what had happened to him as a writer between his eighth-grade year, when he held such promise, and his senior year, when he was in a class for remedial readers and writers. After several months of probing, prodding, and pushing Bryan to examine his writing process, he entered Carol's class one day and began talking about a collaborative story he had to write for another English class. They talked about his frustrations and, when he completed the assigned short story, Carol asked Bryan to write a reflection about the process. This later became an introduction to his portfolio and a portion of a manuscript that they plan to submit for publication.

> Imagine, if you will, being a student named Bryan and walking into your English composition classroom on any given day. The ritual is always the same: walk in, sit down, and await your next assignment. But today is different. Today your teacher asks the class to begin to count off by fives and group with your corresponding number. Once the group has gathered together your teacher announces your assignment. Collaborate!
>
> Collaborate on what, you ask both yourself and the four others sentenced to this foreboding and impending doom. You are to collaborate on writing a short story, possibly with four people with whom you have nothing in common, do not know, and do not really care to collaborate on anything with them (let alone a short story).
>
> You decide that since your grade rides on this seemingly fruitless activity, you should begin to toss around a few ideas for a story. You recall a great idea which you have been mulling over about a man who, betrayed by his own

conscience, must come to grips with the futility of the pointless murder he has committed. This character must come to realize the difference between good and evil before it's too late to save himself.

Your partners have different ideas.

One person has this wonderful idea for a story about a train engineer who must deliver a letter before noon the next day. He must face many obstacles on the way such as: a complete lack of purpose, bad characterization, and the attention span of Boo Radley. He misses his deadline and, like all good characters do, he goes insane and rams his train through a building. He and all of the inhabitants perish in flames.

Another of your collaborators wishes to write a love story. The classic love story of boy meets girl; boy loves girl; girl loves boy; but mean father refuses to allow their love to blossom. Boy and girl elope and form a suicide pact. Boy inherits $100 million from a dead uncle; dad reconsiders; so boy, girl, and good old dad live happily ever after.

A third member of the group suggests that you write a love story about a man and this train. Are you beginning to see the point?

The complete lack of a unified idea causes chaos. No one will make suggestions any longer because they are shot down by frustrated writers whose ideas are not being used. Nothing is accomplished. The days dwindle down and the next thing you know, the assignment is due in twenty-four hours and nothing good has been written yet.

This is when you take matters into your own hands and decide to write the story yourself! You tell the four other members of the group that you will write the story and put each of their names on it.

Bryan wanted desperately to be a writer. He loved the English language, but didn't like English classes. Unfortunately, stories like Bryan's are not unique. An overwhelming number of students who dislike reading and are either adamant about their hatred for writing or have spent years playing the passive resistant role come to us each year. When he reflected on his writing experience for his Chapter I writing portfolio, Bryan was able to sort out the reasons for his negative feelings about collaboration and writing. His English teacher had set the parameters for group work, determined the group members, set time lines for due date and process procedures, and assigned the type of prose to be written. Bryan was frustrated by these steps; they violated his personal writing process. He found that the conditions around which he was to build his success as a writer had actually led him to feel like a failure. Bryan summarized his new understanding of collaboration in the closing reflection of his portfolio:

> Imagine, one more time, if you will, being the skeptical student who, through the completion of a successful collaborative piece [titled "Learning Through Inquiry: A Teacher and Student Collaboration"], now feels at ease with the concept of collaboration. The uneasy feeling has been replaced by the confidence and ability to collaborate once again if the need arises. Although

you still feel most comfortable with solitary writing (and still do not foresee fictional collaboration as a project), you begin to see the need for collaborative writing. You realize that by collaborating with the right person they could become the antithesis to your writing deficiencies. In nonfiction writing, the truth is told (as opposed to the fantasy world of fiction where anything goes) and having a partner to share the research and workload can sometimes be quite a brilliant idea (sometimes, though, it can be a brilliant mistake) that adds both depth and insight to the project.

If Bryan had been a student in Carol's class during the previous year, when she was still administering traditional final exams, he would not have gained the personal insights he gained using a portfolio. The portfolio allowed Bryan the opportunity to reflect on his learning.

The type of insight Bryan gained during his last weeks of high school, when he wrote his reflective narrative, would have happened only by chance, if at all, as a student in Carol's eighth-grade language-arts class. Bryan and his classmates merely went back to their writing folders and chose their best pieces to display in their portfolios. At that time, Carol's approach to portfolios and their use was limited by her understanding of the learning process.

Many educators are weary of hearing that portfolios are the latest trend in education; they say that portfolios have been part of education for many years. English teachers have often used writing folders, and some teachers and school districts have even called these portfolios. However, few have been used for purposes beyond accountability. In the past, portfolios were comprised of pieces of writing used by a department head or principal to check on the amount of writing that teachers assigned their English classes. In some cases, the papers were kept as proof to parents that writing had been taught. (Most often these folders collected dust and presented a storage problem.)

Actors, models, makeup artists, advertising agents, photographers, and architects are professionals who use a portfolio to highlight talents and abilities. Once these professionals acquire their job, however, the portfolio is safely stored away until needed to showcase talents for the next job. If a portfolio is only a storage tool for classroom artifacts or a display case for professional talents, it could be compared to the shoe box that Carol has in her attic and Janell has on the top shelf of her closet containing souvenirs from high school. Many of the yellowed and crumbled items have sentimental value but have lost the significance they once held because we did not record our thoughts to store along with our collection of treasures.

We first considered using portfolios with our students because, as a tool for assessment, portfolios had the potential to answer the question of evaluation for the process-oriented teacher. We spent nearly eighteen weeks of the Chapter I Reading/Writing Lab developing an interactive community, helping students take risks and responsibility for their learning. Choice had been an integral part of the reading, writing, and speaking experiences, and many reflective activities had strengthened our process awareness.

We were fearful that we might destroy the tentative steps our students had begun to take in their learning if we administered the traditional paper-and-pencil test required at the end of the semester. The individual paths our students had followed in their pursuit of learning could not be scored by a Scantron machine located in a teacher's workroom in some other part of the building. Our old methods of assessing learning simply did not work any longer. Our understanding of learning had changed, and we needed new assessment measures that reflected those changes.

The easiest way to illustrate the assessment dilemma we faced is to share the stories of three of our students. Carol first thought about Doug; he had a history of learning problems that had hampered him throughout his schooling. As a result, Doug spent many years in self-contained learning disability (LD) classes. Final exams caused Doug extreme anxiety, but portfolio use allowed him to describe and display his experimentation with writing. One of Doug's goals was to write in a paragraph format. Doug and Carol discovered that his use of 3" x 5" cards to jot down ideas into categories was helpful not only for his order of presentation; he was also able to *see* the need for paragraphs.

Another strategy that Doug used in his writing began when he received his peer response cards from authors' circle. By taping the cards to his computer monitor after pulling his rough draft onto the screen for revision, shown in Figure 2-1, Doug was able to see not only where the content needed to be changed, but said, for the first time, he could understand the need for change. The portfolio, unlike the final exam, was a vehicle for Doug to review his experimentation and development as a writer and discover strategies he could apply to other learning situations.

Jason entered Carol's classroom with the loud proclamation that he couldn't read, so he didn't see any need to be in her class since he hadn't learned after eleven years of schooling. His journal entries for *Don't Look Behind You* by Lois Duncan (the first book that the class read) caused Carol to be concerned that Jason's self-assessment might be accurate, but she also wondered if the literature discussions would provide the support needed to clear up his confusion.

When Jason wrote in response to the first chapter in *Don't Look Behind You*, (see Figure 2-2) he was confused and wanted to know "wates hir father involed in" (what's her father involved in). His question format looked like an easy way for Jason to find out about the story without reading, a technique that he put in place whenever reading was involved.

After Jason's Chapter 5 journal entry, shown in Figure 2-3, Carol was encouraged both by his statement that April shouldn't have opened the door and by

Figure 2-1.

his feelings toward Max. Carol wrote back to Jason asking why he did not trust Max, hoping Jason would provide some facts he had used in his interpretation. Once again, it appeared that Jason had taken the easy way out by simply changing his mind; however, after another question, he stated that the way Max treated the Vamp was his reason for his distrust.

By Chapter 18, Jason was questioning the author's decision to have the car battery run down at the climax of the story (see Figure 2-4). Obviously Jason was not only reading, but he was posing genuine questions and developing the confidence and strategies that all readers need.

Jason might have been happier with an objective final exam. After all, he didn't need to read the material on such a test, he just needed to mark answers. When Jason chose these responses for his portfolio, he discovered he was, indeed, a reader who now needed to understand the strategies he was using and could use to become more confident.

Laura was placed in our program by her social worker with the hope that she could find a community where she would feel comfortable enough to speak. Early attempts to pull her into our literature circles were futile. Initially, Laura stood in the back room where we stored our books and stared at the shelves of paperbacks for the entire hour. This way she avoided any contact with the class under the guise of searching for the perfect book. Eventually, students joined Laura and recommended their favorite books to her.

cafter 1   Jason

~~xxxxxxxxxxxxxxxxxxxxxx~~

I dont under sated
wate happend;
it confosing.
wates his father
in voled in

I had the same
question Jason.
Did you read the
back cover — that's
what I did to try
to figure out what
he was doing.

What do you think
was confusing?

I was but sins
I raid on omy not

Figure 2-2

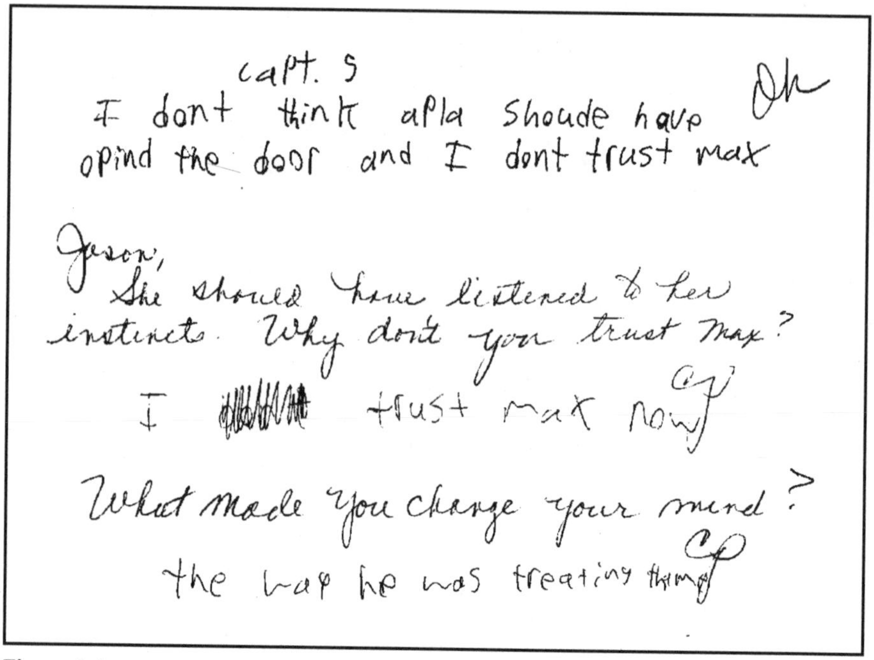
capt. 5
I dont think apla shoude have opind the door and I dont trust max
Oh
Jason,
She should have listened to her instincts. Why don't you trust Max?
I trust max now
CP
What made you change your mind?
the way he was treating them
CP

Figure 2-3.

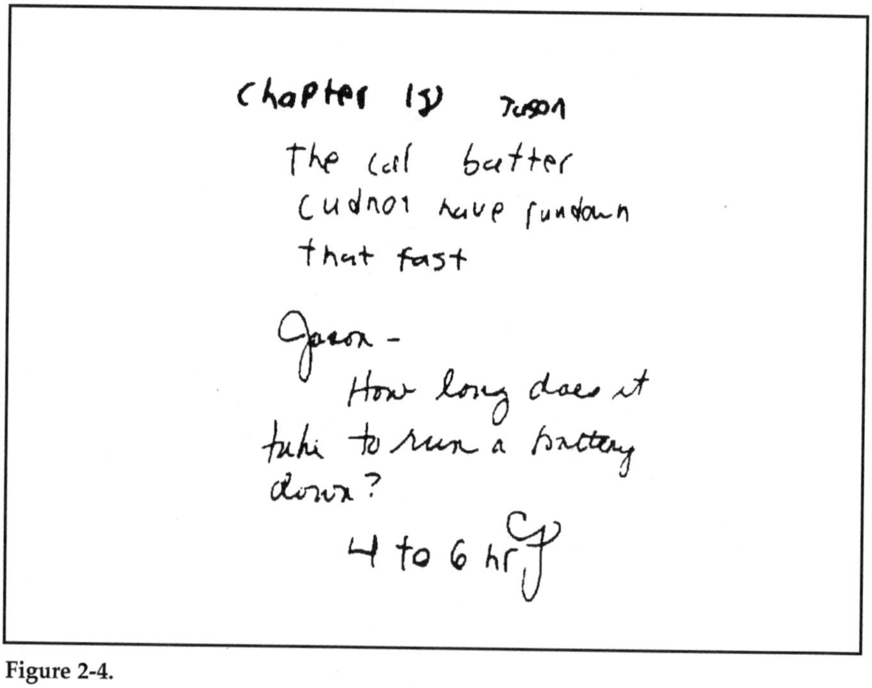
Chapter 13 Jason
The car batter cudnot have rundown that fast
Jason -
How long does it take to run a battery down?
4 to 6 hr
CP

Figure 2-4.

When she finally emerged with a book in hand, *The Third Eye* by Lois Duncan, Shauna, who had recommended it, volunteered to discuss it with her through written conversation. All Laura had to do was leave a note for Shauna in her folder and she would respond.

The minute she entered class, Laura would run to her folder to see if she had a note from her newly found reading partner. Eventually, Shauna suggested that they just discuss the book orally because she had forgotten to write but she felt like talking about the book. Laura took the bait and developed into a voracious reader, frequently checking out two novels for weekend reading sessions.

By the end of the first semester, Laura read her first piece of writing to our authors' circle. Every class member felt a sense of pride. How could a semester exam reveal what Laura and her classmates had discovered about learning? We had all grown from our contact with Laura. We began to see the impact that our involvement with and excitement about learning could have on those around us. Several students not only mentioned Laura in their portfolios, but also included written conversation they had with her as we tried to pull her into our community of learners.

Since these first portfolios were an alternative to semester exams, we asked students to collect and organize all their semester work. We then asked them to analyze that work by responding to a list of questions we had composed. Although we acknowledged that we had taken a step in the right direction, we soon realized that we really hadn't moved very far beyond the writing folder we talked about earlier. We still had no plans to use the answers to the questions we posed. We began to question how we could move beyond the "accountability" folder. As with all the activities, strategies, and experiences we consider for and with our students, our first concern was the authenticity of the portfolios our students were creating. We wondered if we could find examples of portfolio use in our everyday lives that might help clarify their potential value and use beyond accountability.

Carol found, in the pantry of her kitchen, a "portfolio" that was, in fact, her Aunt Jo's cookbook. Although its outside appearance resembled any other cookbook, inside the covers Aunt Jo's experimentation, problem solving, and personality emerge from her years of cooking at the convent in Peoria, Illinois. The margins hold special messages of changes in ingredients, comments from guests who tasted the creation, and occasions when the recipe was served. Some pages hold news clippings that have been tucked inside the book next to the original recipe. These newspaper articles not only describe the awards that she won at the Heart of Illinois Fair, but the quotes gathered by news reporters captured her reflections and the goals she had set for herself. Although never called a portfolio, Aunt Jo's cookbook explored her learning process and celebrated her achievements, as seen in Figures 2–5 and 2–6.

Mom's, **Baked Spaghetti**

7 qt. water	White brick cheese,
2 1/2 T. salt	1 1/4 lb. sliced (do not
1/4 c. Mazola oil	substitute any other kind
1 1/2 lb. spaghetti	of cheese)

To cook spaghetti use 8-quart kettle and add water, salt, and oil; let come to a boil. Add spaghetti; stir occasionally with long fork and cook until tender, 15 to 20 minutes. Do not put under cold water as the oil takes the starch out of the spaghetti. Drain spaghetti well.

Baked spaghetti: Grease an 11x15-inch pan. Put a layer of meat sauce, then a layer of spaghetti and mix well; keep repeating with each layer. Then on last layer of spaghetti and sauce. Put slices of white brick cheese and cover again with a thinner layer of sauce. Bake in a preheated oven at 350° for 40 to 45 minutes. Then take out of the oven and set on top of stove range about 20 minutes. Cut into squares and serve in the pan.

Note: fresh, left-over sauce serves 10 to 15.

To seal in juices lap slices of cheese over each other.

Sr. Concepta Marie Nydo

Our special treat to look forward to the holidays. Mouth watering and so delicious!

If you haven't met the devil face-to-face,
maybe you're going the same way he is.

Figure 2-5.

Champion pie baker

A 'blue ribbon' nun

SISTER CONCEPTA Marie said she uses her own recipes, and she learned to cook by herself, mainly trying things on her own while in the novitiate.

"I used to watch my mother. But she only let me watch. She told me if she let me try and I spoiled it, we wouldn't have any."

She has reached her present level of expertise in the culinary arts through experimenting, she said. "They say practice makes perfect," she noted.

The judges at the Heart of Illinois Fair and the residents of the Immaculate Conception Convent would probably agree that practice has definitely paid off in Sister Concepta Marie's case.

Figure 2-6.

Only recently did we realize that one of the most obvious examples of portfolios was just outside our office door. Each Monday our office partner, Mike, set up the television and VCR in the small workroom adjoining our office and began examining the films from Saturday's football game (see Figure 2-7). As head football coach, it was his job to reflect on the performances of the coaches and team and, most importantly, determine what needed to be done before the next game. His goal to build a winning football program was centered on evaluating what individuals could do, capitalizing on their strengths, and setting team and personal goals to overcome weaknesses.

Armed with these "real life" examples, our year's experimentation, and the learning stories of students like Bryan, Doug, Jason, and Laura, our personal definition of portfolio began to evolve. We decided that a portfolio is comprised of a collection of artifacts accompanied by a reflective narrative that not only helps the learner to understand and extend learning, but invites the reader of the portfolio to gain insights about learning and the learner. However, the words of caution from Donald Graves, author of *Writing: Teachers and Children at Work,* in his May 1990 address to the International Reading Association (IRA) convention in Atlanta, suggesting that educators needed to take an experimental stance with portfolios comforted us, yet pushed us to find out as much as we could. We tried to find sources that would validate and stimulate our thinking on the potential of portfolios. At that time only a few journal articles were available. The one we found most helpful was "Portfolio Assessment: Sampling Student Work" by Dennie Palmer Wolf (1986), which reinforced the need to question traditional assessment instruments. Our discussion of her article prompted us to devise a chart that contrasted the differences between traditional assessment and what we were beginning to see as nontraditional assessment.

TRADITIONAL ASSESSMENTS	NONTRADITIONAL ASSESSMENTS
Focus on skill performance	Focus on process
Students acquire objective knowledge	Students thoughtfully judge their own work
Achievement matters	Development matters
Teacher's responsibility	Shared responsibility
First and only draft work valued	Multiple drafts valued
Used to determine a grade	Used by student and teacher to guide learning

We then went back to our students' portfolios and analyzed them to determine if there was a match between what we said we believed about learning and what we were beginning to value in assessment. Were our students' portfolios focusing on process, for example, and were students thoughtfully

Figure 2-7.

judging their own work? We focused on Tracey's portfolio for this analysis since we both shared a history with her and we had that "gut" feeling that the change in instruction was working for Tracey.

Tracey, like Bryan, had been one of Carol's eighth-grade language-arts students. As a freshman, she was Janell's English student. Tracey enrolled in the Chapter I Reading/Writing Lab when she was a senior. From the time Tracey had entered her early teens, she constantly battled the tension of wanting to be her own kind of person. She realized, however, that the decisions she made while trying to achieve this goal might isolate her from her peers within the classroom setting and in her personal life. As a result, revision of her writing was seen as a personal threat and a criticism of her abilities as a writer. She was also reluctant to share her opinions about her reading. Carol recalls a stand off that she and Tracey had in eighth grade concerning Tracey's attitude about discussing a novel she was reading. "I'll sit with the group while they discuss the book Mrs. Porter, but you can't make me talk about it," Tracey said as a compromise a week after her first refusal to attend literature discussion. Even as a senior, Tracey still struggled with letting others support her learning. She would have been characterized by most of her teachers as "average," but the reflections in her portfolio that she wrote as a third person narrative display anything but an average reader and writer.

Once upon a time, there was a girl named Tracey (that's me). Tracey was sitting in study hall one day when Mrs. Porter (her eighth grade English teacher) entered. Mrs. Porter called off several names, one of which was Tracey's, and began to talk about a reading writing class she had that she felt would benefit Tracey and several students. Mrs. Porter explained it would be very similar to the class Tracey had with Mrs. Porter in eighth grade. Remembering how much fun the class was Tracey accepted the invitation.

The following day Tracey entered her new third hour classroom. Only a few students occupied the dozen or so desks that made a circle in the middle of the room. Mrs. Cleland (Tracey's freshman year English teacher) was the instructor for this hour.

After several days of reading short stories, the students were given the assignment of interviewing another student. It was Tracey's job to interview Jimmy Gonzales. With knowing very little about Jimmy and his life, Tracey thought up some very interesting questions. She did know that Jimmy was a vital person in MHS's state-championship gymnastics team. So, one day Tracey was reading an article about Boris Shakhliln and Tracey got the idea of Jimmy beating Boris and winning the championship.

The hardest part of writing the article was getting the first few words, in the correct order, down on paper. Later Tracey found there was no "correct" or "wrong" way about the order of her words. After pulling her piece out of the computer printer Tracey brought it to author's circle. There she read her piece out-loud to the class and they offered suggestions and asked questions about unclear sentences or paragraphs. Tracey left the circle and revised her piece.

Tracey's favorite piece was a piece she began when she was still in Mrs. Cleland's class. Tracey needed a quick piece to read to the class and she didn't have any ideas. One night when she was laying in bed Tracey got her idea. With only the dim light her desk lamp gave off, Tracey began writing about her vacation. She couldn't find any paper so she searched under her bed and found her progress reports to use.

Tracey's best piece ended up being her most revised piece with 26 revisions (and still going). Beginning it in late October Tracey feels she is just about ready to resubmit it to a magazine, it's now early June! Considering this is her best piece, Tracey put forth a lot of effort, emotion, and time to make this piece be just perfect. Several teachers and friends read her "Lennie" piece and added comments and suggestions to make it even better (see Appendix A).

Currently as a writer, Tracey still gets frustrated at getting the ideas and getting the initial words down on paper. She gets her ideas by sitting and looking at an old tree or watching her little cousin run in the yard. When she begins her revision process, Tracey no longer just tears it out of the printer and rushes to the authors' circle, she tears it out and reads it. By the time the authors' circle hears it, it is usually her fourth or fifth draft! Her best piece differs from her first piece because of the effort she puts forth and the time she spent revising. One last observation Tracey wants to share is that she no longer feels her writing is always correct as it is. She is open more to suggestions. She has grown as a writer because she is much more willing to listen to people as critics.

Her first journal entries were in the form of bookmarks. Tracey was given a small piece of paper and told she was to write her feelings and comments about the book. Her first entries were frustrating because Tracey was used to picking up a book, reading it, and then finding another book. Now Tracey was expected to share her thoughts. What would she say?

After reading several books and keeping journals, Tracey read the Wizard of Oz. It was the fantasy unit and Tracey didn't want to read a book with anyone in her class so she chose a book she knew no one would have thought of. Because the libraries didn't have a copy on hand of the Oz Tracey went out and bought the last copy in a local bookstore. Tracey is a Wizard of Oz movie freak! Every year Tracey would have her TV turned on to the Oz. As she began to read the book she noted the severe differences from the book and the movie. Tracey was very disappointed in the book!

As a reader the only frustrations Tracey has is stopping in the middle of the book to write down her feelings. Tracey had always been the type of person who reads and that's it. She'll use her own experiences to understand a character, or she'll put a face with a character but she still has a problem with writing down her feelings at the end of each chapter. Before the lab, Tracey would read anything with a neat cover or anything by V.C. Andrews. She is still a fan of V.C. Andrews but she no longer judges a book by its cover. In the beginning if she didn't understand something she was reading she would just reread it but now, if she still doesn't understand it, there is usually someone she can discuss it with.

Well, it's now time for Tracey to do her portfolio. The year is over but as a reader and writer Tracey knows she will carry what she has learned with her throughout the summer and her life.

Had we not known better we would have thought that Tracey had collaborated with Dennie Wolf to show that students need to be "thoughtful respondents to, and judges of, their own work" (35). We checked and rechecked the chart comparing traditional and nontraditional assessment (see page 23) that we had scribbled on a scrap of paper somewhere in one of our portfolio folders. Tracey's reflective narrative displayed each of the goals we were attempting to reach by using portfolios as a nontraditional assessment. We decided to make a neater copy of the chart to use as a framework for decisionmaking and further research with our next set of portfolios.

In the traditional classroom the *focus is on skill performance*. Frank Smith calls the traditional view of learning "memorization," and the assessment that most closely matches this form of instruction is the traditional test that requires students to show how much and to what degree they have memorized (1986). When tests are written for students in this type of classroom, the purpose is to determine if the student has learned what has been taught.

The nontraditional assessment instrument allows learners to *focus on their process*. Learners examine the unique paths they followed while authoring ideas; the self-knowledge that emerges helps them adapt to new situations by revealing learning strategies and helping them to establish goals for future experiences.

By reflecting in her portfolio, Tracey discovered that "there was no 'correct' or 'wrong' way about the order of her words." She uses authors' circle as a way to revise her rough drafts, but her writing process changes over the course of the year. Initially, Tracey "pulled her piece out of the computer printer" and "brought it to author's circle." Later in the school year Tracey "no longer just tears it out of the printer and rushes to the authors' circle, she tears it out and reads it. By the time the authors' circle hears it, it is usually her fourth or fifth draft!" Many of our students refer to this new development in Tracey's process as being able to "do authors' circle in your head."

Acquiring objective knowledge is the purpose of learning in the traditional classroom. This fact is what prompts students to ask the famous, "Will this be on the test?" question during instruction. When students receive low test scores, it simply indicates that students have not learned the information taught in that specific setting, although the implications for individual students may go beyond that conclusion.

In the nontraditional classroom *students thoughtfully judge their own work.* They go back to previous assignments and analyze the changes, determining what caused change, and then set goals for future experiences based upon that analysis.

Tracey believes that her best piece is indicative of the "effort, emotion, and time" that went into making it "perfect," even though she states that she is still revising. Tracey set new goals for herself as a writer by choosing from several of the comments and suggestions she received on her *Lennie* piece.

Achievement matters in the traditional classroom. Teachers keep score and that score is based upon how many facts the student was able to memorize in preparation for the test. Comparisons are made between students, classes, schools, and districts. These comparisons are based upon how much the student has "learned" in terms of facts or skills.

Development matters in the nontraditional classroom. Judgments are not made in relation to mastery of facts or skills, and students are not compared to each other or ranked according to the correctness with which they responded to questions. The individual growth in knowledge and development of abilities are valued and serve as bench marks for the future experiences and inquiries of students.

Tracey's development as a writer is at the heart of her entire reflection. Unlike Bryan, who wrote the collaborative piece on his own and then put the group member's names at the top of the page because their "grade rides on this seemingly fruitless activity," Tracey revised her *Lennie* piece for the twenty-sixth time after the four or five revisions that occurred before authors' circle.

Assessment is the *teacher's responsibility* in the traditional classroom. From the time when new facts or skills are presented to the students the teacher takes responsibility for the learning. Presentation of the material, activities to promote memorization, encouragement for success, and assessment instruments are developed by the teacher.

In the nontraditional classroom, assessment is a *shared responsibility*. The process of sorting through and examining the artifacts of learning, then trying to make their own sense out of it through self-evaluation begins with the learners. The teacher's role is that of facilitator.

The reading and writing strategies made available to Tracey throughout the semester were facilitated by her teachers. Tracey personalized authors' circle and literature discussion to meet her needs as a learner. She now sees her teachers and friends as able to help her as a writer rather than feeling like they are criticizing her. Through her self-evaluation, Tracey reveals that writing comments about her reading is a frustrating experience. Although her teachers believe that Tracey will benefit from responding to her reading in writing, and they will assist her in acquiring new strategies, Tracey will also have to share this responsibility.

First and only draft work is valued in the traditional classroom. Assessment instruments using a true/false and multiple choice format do not value the drafting of ideas. In the case of short-answer or essay tests, the student is usually required to draft an answer within the time frame of the test. More often than not there is no time or opportunity for revision of ideas or creating a final draft on these assessment instruments.

Multiple drafts are valued in the nontraditional classroom. The learners' process, from the inception of an idea to the final product, is examined because with each revision the students are beginning to understand their own style, to analyze their audience, and to work for additional detail. Students examine these drafts to determine the strategies that have helped them become better readers, writers, speakers, and listeners.

Each of the twenty-six drafts of *Lennie* that Tracey included in her portfolio revealed a wealth of information regarding Tracey's writing process. She was able to compare and contrast her early revisions, which focused on correcting mechanics, to the drafts that she wrote once she decided to submit the piece for publication. With her change in purpose and audience, Tracey's revisions focused on enhancing visual images and creating an ending that forced the reader to consider the impact of the Lennies in their lives.

The assessment instrument in the traditional classroom is *used to determine a grade*. Again, the teacher is trying to find out how much material the student has assimilated. The difference between known and unknown information is translated into a score or grade. In most classrooms, the test marks the end of a unit of study, and those students who "didn't get it" or "didn't try hard enough" simply receive a lower grade and move on with the rest of the students. Seldom are traditional tests used to determine future learning experiences.

In contrast to traditional assessment where learning is seen as complete when a test has been given, the nontraditional viewpoint is that learning is never complete. Therefore, assessment is *used to guide learning*. One experience leads to another that leads to a new learner, who is guided by an ongoing need to set and obtain new reading and writing goals. When students and teachers use the portfolio to determine what caused them to change, they can use this new information to determine future learning experiences.

Tracey's reflections provide a wealth of information to guide both the teacher and Tracey in her future learning. Together they can build on her strengths, which include an understanding and appreciation of her writing process and her development as a writer. Tracey does not have the same insights about herself as a reader. She is beginning to see reading as a process, but she is hesitant and frustrated with understanding that discussion and writing are strategies that can support her development. Tracey's reflections on her reading process give her teacher feedback on instruction. If writing in response to reading isn't working for Tracey, an examination of alternative strategies might need to be made.

The comparison of traditional and nontraditional assessments and analyzing student reflections such as Tracey's was the confirmation and foundation we needed to move forward with our portfolio experimentation. We now understood that assessment needed to match the beliefs we had about learning, which in turn was reflected in our classroom instruction and informed by the assessment instruments being used.

With many of our questions concerning assessment answered, we then tried to correlate the purposes and values we had established for portfolios in our classrooms with those that exist in real world portfolios. Our confidence plummeted. Carol's aunt had not created her cookbook portfolio because she was trying to find an alternative to testing. Her portfolio had been a part of her learning; it supported her growth and celebrated her successes. This insight gave us a new direction to consider for our inquiry; it further supported our feeling that we needed to explore the use of portfolios beyond assessment. We generated the following questions to guide our next portfolio experience:

- How can portfolios be used to support learning?
- If the portfolio is supporting learning, where can it take the learner in future learning experiences?
- How can portfolios be used to celebrate development?

Appendix A: It Was The Biggest Buck I Ever Saw

Lennie

After a ten hour car ride, the last thing any 16 year old girl, especially me, would want to do is go to a bar. But, after a short series of "I don't knows" and "Doesn't matter to me's," my father, cousin Jerry, his son Skyler, and I climbed into the old clunking "Bingo Mobile." This Tank-turned-car should have been junked after World War I! It rattled all the way down the dirt and gravel road to our destination. Climbing out of the depths of the back seat (after what appeared to be a never ending ride), we entered Jackson's Hole. Definitely not Minnesota's finest!

This badly lit bar had a ten-point buck head with antlers hung over the door to welcome me. The usual drunks were slumped over the bar, smelling of last week's alcohol. Through the thick, gray smoke and crowd we fought our way to a table in a far back corner. Immediately I began to use my short fingernails to flake away what appeared to be hardened chocolate pudding that some considerate customer had left behind.

Searching the room, through the thick haze of cigarette smoke, I noticed nothing had changed since my last vacation, 3 months before. The same corners contained the same large, spread-out cobwebs with most likely the same flies stuck to them. An old-fashioned horse harness hung beside an ax, both to gather dust on the wall directly behind us. The jukebox belted out the native country music so loudly I could barely hear the bleached-blond waitress ask me (between gum chops) what I wanted to drink. Over the verse, "There is deer in my beer. . ." I shouted, "A Pepsi, please." Continuing to scan the room, I noticed those blue Finish eyes staring. Sagging skin, a long pointed nose, and a mess of curly, dirty-blonde hair surrounded those huge eyes. I knew it had to be Lennie! He was staring intensely at me, trying to place my face with my name. I had met Lennie before! He's an old family friend and unfortunately the biggest BS'er on the west side of Lake Superior. He could tell you a story about anything from his Uncle Uno's false teeth chattering on the table, to the time he shot and killed the ghost deer, which only he could see when he was plastered. Quickly I looked away. Maybe if I don't look at him, he wouldn't realize who I was. I looked up! I couldn't help it!

Sure enough "Howdy Doody" himself strutted over toward our table in his cowboy boots and bright neon-orange hunting shirt. His shining silver belt buckle and worn leather belt held up his faded jeans, which were too big for his skinny old-mannish body. Although my father, 42, is six years older than Lennie, Lennie still shouted, "Willie, my boy! . . . I see you brought along your daughter." Jerry and Skyler began to moan for now we wouldn't ever get rid of him!

Lennie slapped my dad on the back with all the power that he could, then placed his beer firmly on the table, as if he was telling a dog to stay. Reaching over the table, Lennie attempted, in his drunken state, to pat everyone on the head. As he reached for me, Lennie knocked over his beer, the glass shattered, and the beer splashed all over the table! "Damn Chinese!" Lennie shouted. Like usual. Lennie blamed his clumsiness on someone else. "They keep making this cheap @*&!" Embarrassed, he stumbled off in his drunken state in search of another beer. I was relieved! Our bimbo waitress came to wipe up Lennie's mess but ended up wiping half of the beer onto our laps with her blackened dish rag. As soon as the waitress left, back came Lennie, weaving around people, chairs, and tables with his beer mug held high and steady to be sure not to spill a drop. He had himself focused on our table, like a weasel drawn to a chicken coup. "Let's start this again," he shouted in our ears.

I knew we would be there until midnight listening to Lennie's tales, but for some reason I didn't care! This trip had started out just like the last one, and I had a great time then, too!

"So, anyway last night I was looking out of the living room window, of the house I built with my own two hands, no help from anyone," Lennie began with a heavy sigh. If Lennie heard the moans from Skyler he only used them as an inspiration to continue. "He tells this one every year." Skyler added. I couldn't help but laugh to myself. Lennie's tales were something I didn't get to hear very often, although they were always the same, I missed them! I turned to Lennie and listened attentively to his story. Without any hesitation Lennie looked directly at me and continued, "I saw this huge buck. It was the biggest buck I've ever saw . . ."

I like portfolios. I love the idea of letting other people read my pieces and giving their thoughts about them. It gives me a chance to hear other peoples comment. I also like the idea of letting us show our growth to the teachers. (not having the teachers telling us what she/he felt about our writing and what we need to work on). I like looking at other peoples writings. It gives me a chance to see what other people are doing. Portfolios also give me a first hand view of what I need to work on and what I should keep on doing.

Rebecca

THROUGH OUR CONVERSATIONS while drafting the ideas for each chapter, and by reviewing journal entries such as Becky's, shown here, we began to realize that reflection had become so automatic in our classrooms that we did not truly appreciate the important role it had played as we formulated our ideas about portfolios. Students reflected on their writing process during their conferences with us; they reflected on the reading strategies that had been most effective for them at the end of a novel; and we had incorporated process share days when students helped one another see the strategies they were using in their reading and writing. Students reflected at the end of a day, at the end of the week, at the end of the grading period—it was a way of life in our classrooms. At one point our students even suggested we have class T-shirts printed that said *Reflect*.

As we shared ideas for this chapter around each others' kitchen tables, we realized that the title of this chapter should really be "How Can Reflection Be Used to Support Learning?" It was our belief in the power of reflection that helped us move beyond seeing the portfolio as a mere alternative to traditional assessment to appreciating its value as a learning strategy. In this capacity, portfolios become vehicles for reflection in which learners examine where they have been, where they are now, how they got there, and where they need to go next. Linda Crafton states, "When learners have a chance to reflect on their reading\writing\language experiences, they can assume an altered stance on their learning and see it in a new way. They also become aware of and learn to value the strategies they are developing" (1991, 314). Our commitment to reflection was further supported by the American Psychological Association (APA) in their development of twelve "Learner-Centered Principles" resulting from the recent research in psychology relevant to education. The APA suggests that higher order strategies for "thinking about thinking" facilitate creative and critical thinking and the development of expertise. Learners' awareness of their personal control over thinking and learning processes promotes higher levels of commitment, persistence, and involvement in learning. Reflection can provide a place for the learner to exercise that control over their own thinking (1992).

A colleague from a neighboring school district helped us to further appreciate the value of ongoing reflection. Several months after hearing us speak at a local conference, she called Janell and asked her to stop by and look at her first portfolio attempt. She was disappointed and needed some reassurance that she was moving in the right direction. She explained that the portfolios looked beautiful; the students had spent hours designing and creating them, but they just didn't "say anything." When Janell asked her how often the students wrote reflections during the school year, there was a long pause. Finally, she responded with, "I don't know whether to be embarrassed or relieved. How could I expect them to provide valuable insight into their learning when this was their first time to write reflections? But at least I know what to do differently this fall." By simply introducing questions such as *What have I done? What am I doing? Why did I change? What remains to be done?* the student and the teacher can begin routinely reflecting on their learning experiences and can make interpretations from those reflections. We need to remind ourselves that reflection is not an end product, therefore, we do not need to wait until the end of the year to reflect on learning experiences. As an ongoing strategy, it can provide learners with valuable insight into their learning processes.

Even though we realized that the questions we asked of our students during our first portfolio efforts were too directive, it is possible that variations of those same questions could be asked to support students in their early attempts at reflection. As the students become more comfortable with reflection as a strategy, they can move away from the questions and create their own narrative response.

Writing

- What frustrations did you have with writing earlier in the year and how has that changed?

- What currently frustrates you as a writer?
- How did you come up with ideas for writing?
- How do you decide on ideas now?
- How did you revise pieces of writing earlier this year?
  (For example, rewording, adding content [details, expanding ideas, examples], rearranging, fixing mechanical problems . . .)
- How do you revise now?
- How is your first piece of writing different from your best piece?
- What makes your best piece best?
- How do you write for an audience now, compared to the way you used to consider the audience while writing?
- Are there any other observations you would like to share with us?

Reading

- What frustrations did you have with reading earlier in the year and how has that changed?
- What currently frustrates you as a reader?
- Prior to this class, how did you choose what you would read?
- How do you choose now?
- What did you do at the beginning of the year to help you understand your reading?
- What helps you understand your reading now?
- What made your favorite piece of reading different from other books you have read?
- Are there any other observations you would like to share with us?

After a year of reading and responding to our students' reflections, we decided to analyze their responses to determine exactly what we could learn about our students through their reflections. This list is certainly not inclusive, but represents what we have discovered in our classrooms. We found that reflection allows students to

- examine their learning process.
- take responsibility for their own learning.
- see "gaps" in their learning.
- determine strategies that support their learning.
- celebrate risk-taking and inquiry.
- set goals for future experiences.
- see changes and development over time.

By sharing some of the student reflections that helped us generate our list of categories, we can illustrate the importance of drawing conclusions from student reflections.

REFLECTION ALLOWS LEARNERS TO EXAMINE THEIR LEARNING PROCESS

When students reflect on and interpret their learning experiences, paths for personal inquiry about learning emerge. No longer are students completing an assignment for the teacher or the letter grade or because they will need specific information or skills when they get to a higher grade level. Instead, they are motivated by the need to satisfy their individual inquiries. Through reflection, students are able to discover how they are different and appreciate the interactions that supported them in their endeavors to understand.

Joe and Desiree were typical Chapter I students who seldom used reading and writing to learn; they went through the motions of completing assignments because that is what students were supposed to do. As they began to read and write for meanings they could create, they began to see that learning was a process.

As Joe reflected on his changes as a reader, he discovered that he was now grouping words while reading, which made his process less frustrating and his reading more interesting (see Figure 3-1). His definition of reading "harder" includes re-reading and discussing with other readers, two strategies that support his understanding. Initially, as teachers, we laughed at Joe's comments about not being able to read when he's hungry, but with Joe's history of reading difficulties, it was crucial for him to discover factors that interfered with his construction of meaning.

From Desiree's reflections on her writing experience she is able to see the reasons for significant change in herself as a learner (see Figure 3-2). Not only has she discovered strategies that will help her as a writer, but she has also changed the way she approaches and views the process. Desiree evolved from a student who completed assignments so she could check them off in her assignment notebook to one who called an authors' circle each time she made revisions to receive feedback on whether or not her most recent changes worked.

REFLECTION ALLOWS LEARNERS TO TAKE RESPONSIBILITY FOR THEIR OWN LEARNING

During the reflective process, the responsibility for learning shifts from teacher to student. Learning becomes a personal responsibility because

I had a hand full of frustrations with my reading earlier in the year. One was that it took me a while to read a book. I feel it shouldn't have taken a normal person like me so long to read a book. I would read a book word by word, not in sections like I have learned to do now. Reading a book in sections makes it much more interesting to the read, than if you read a book word by word like I did in the past. Now when I read a book I just sit down and read till I get hungry. You know you can't read and remember very well if you are hungry.

Toward the end of the year one thing I did to help me understand what I was reading, was to read harder. If I didn't quite understand something I would go back to where the reading began to get confusing, and read over the section that was giving me trouble again. If this wouldn't work, I would talk to someone else who is reading the same book as my class.

Figure 3-1.

MY FIRST PIECE OF Writing I didn't take it SERIOUSLY, WITH The SECOND PIECE I Went through AUThor CirclE twice, this proved to be an effective process because my piece got put up on the board as a piece that had been best revised.

NOW at the end of the semester I look back and compare how my writing has changed. Now I feel I could write anything. You dont have to be good, to be a good writer you just have to be willing to make changes.

Figure 3-2.

self-evaluation determines the instructional decisions made for future learning experiences. This is not something that we, as teachers, can do for or to students. It is the learners' responsibility to sort through and examine the artifacts of their learning, then try to make their own sense out of it. The responsibility for interpretation is theirs.

Beth chose to write in third person the narrative reflections that coordinated the artifacts in her portfolio. She examined her reflections from the first semester and designed a diagram that illustrated her goals for second semester. Periodically she would return to her diagram to check on her progress and reflect on her growth (see Figure 3-3). Jim is no longer depending on a teacher to tell him what to do. He is creating meaning for himself, for the sake of learning, as shown in Figure 3-4.

REFLECTION ALLOWS LEARNERS TO SEE "GAPS" IN THEIR LEARNING

When students and teachers are actively involved in learning, it is sometimes difficult to see areas they have avoided, either intentionally or because they became caught up in something else. Reflection allows us to "step back" from this active involvement and provides the distance we need in order to observe what we were doing as learners. Therefore, reflections can highlight not only what has been done, but what hasn't been done.

In Carol's teaching portfolio she stated:

> When we reached the end of the semester, I realized that many of the students had only completed two novels. We had read a lot of stories which wasn't bad, but for some of the lower-level students that's all they've ever had the chance to read. They needed to become involved in a text, and to do that it required reading material that couldn't be completed in a class period. I've used novels to hook nonreaders before and I can't believe I didn't do it this semester. My students seem to be like me – give me a short story and I can take it or leave it, but give me a good book that can become part of my life for a couple of weeks and it changes me in some way. Obviously, next semester I will go back to what I know has worked before.

If Carol had not taken the time to reflect in her portfolio, she would not have seen the gaps she had created in her own teaching.

When Lisa sat down at the end of the semester, a gap in the amount of reading she had done became immediately obvious. She intended to photocopy the covers of all the books she had read that semester, but she quickly discovered there were very few to choose from; however, her folder was filled with free writing, rough drafts, poetry, and in-progress short stories. Her reflection served as almost a verbal reprimand to herself, one that she heeded during the coming semester when she completed six novels in eighteen weeks (see Figure 3-5).

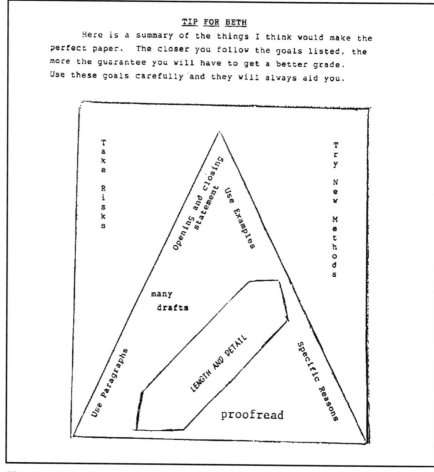

Figure 3-3.

REFLECTION ALLOWS LEARNERS TO DETERMINE STRATEGIES THAT SUPPORTED THEIR LEARNING

Through reflection, learners are able to get inside their thinking to discover the support systems that allowed them to grow; they can become respondents to and judges of their own work (Wolf 1986, 35). The learner creating an autobiography through the use of a portfolio is much like the historian who explores beyond what actually happened in the past. Both the learner and the historian are concerned with interpreting what is known by determining the factors that influenced change.

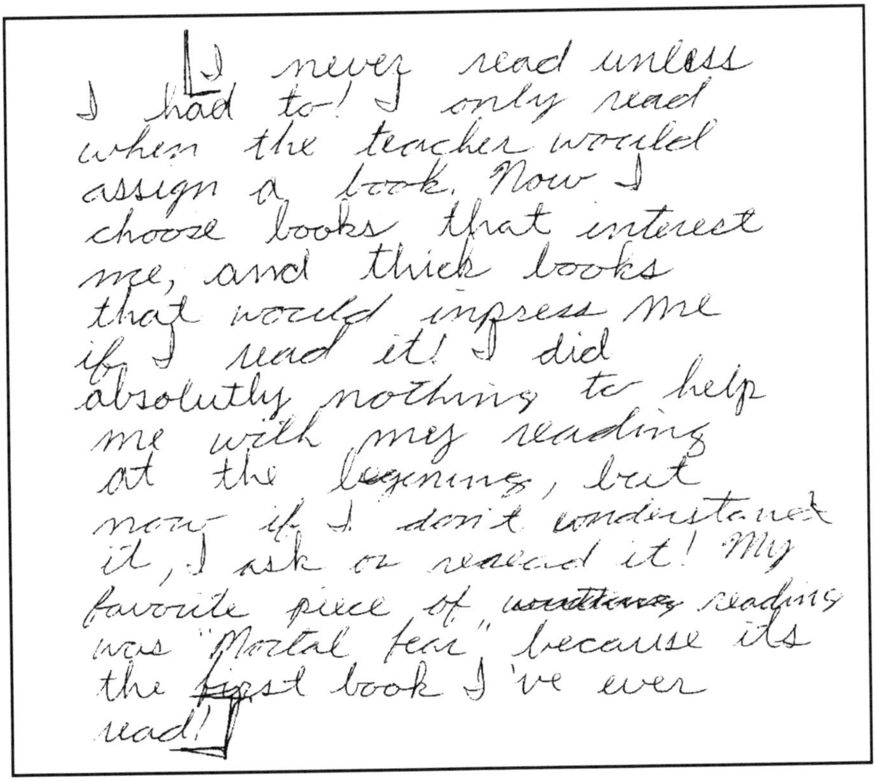

> I never read unless I had to! I only read when the teacher would assign a book. Now I choose books that interest me, and thick books that would impress me if I read it! I did absolutly nothing to help me with my reading at the beginning, but now if I don't understand it, I ask or reread it! My favorite piece of ~~writing~~ reading was "Mortal fear" because its the first book I've ever read!

Figure 3-4.

We all have times in the classroom when, for one reason or another, we relapse to teaching techniques we had long ago abandoned. Janell experienced this "relapse" last spring when she introduced *Romeo and Juliet* to her ninth graders. It was April, and the students had worked the entire school year developing strategies that helped them create personal meaning from their reading. They had been given the freedom to implement the strategies they found most effective. But for some reason, Janell didn't trust those strategies to work with Shakespeare. What if they missed something "important," something that they needed to know to be successful with their next Shakespeare experience?

She abandoned the group discussions which had worked so well on the previous novel and called the students back together as a class of twenty-eight, so she could interpret Shakespeare for them. Within a few days, students were slouching in their desks, complaints were on the rise, and Janell was threatening to administer pop quizzes if the students didn't start reading their assignment. Reflecting at the end of a particularly frustrating week,

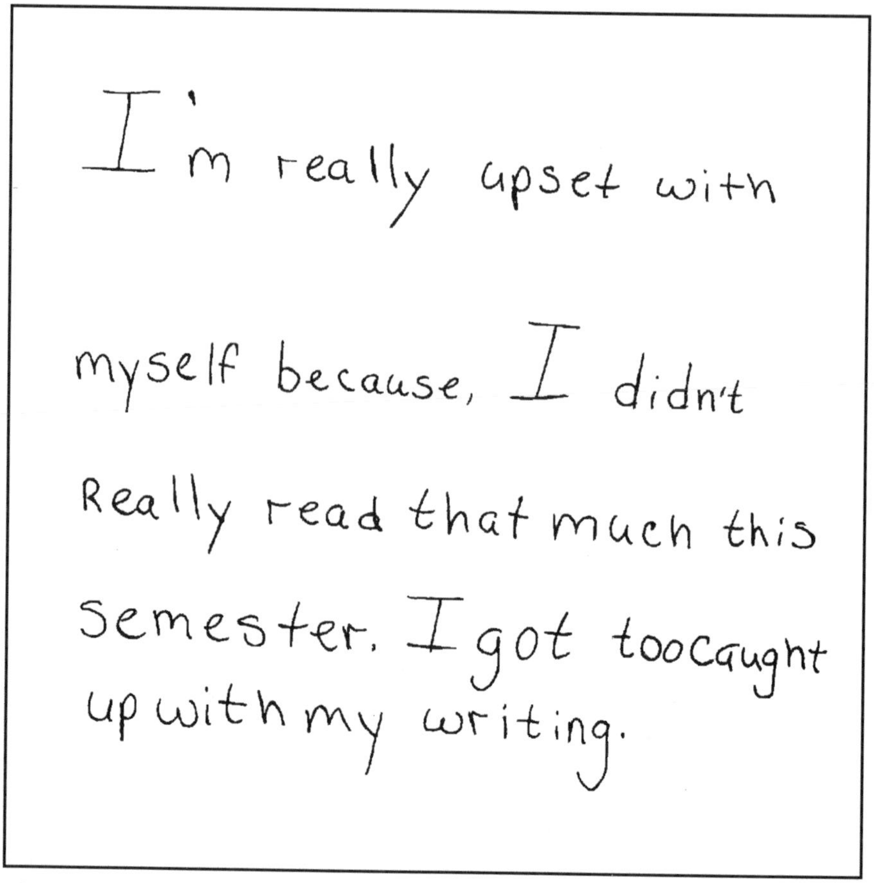

I'm really upset with

myself because, I didn't

Really read that much this

Semester. I got too caught
up with my writing.

Figure 3-5.

Janell finally decided to return to the portfolios the students had assembled in January. She hoped to discover what students felt best-supported their learning and the entries shown in Figures 3-6 and 3-7 provided the help she needed.

Janell had removed the very strategies that would help her students appreciate the beauty of Shakespeare. By Act III they were back on track, thanks to the portfolio reflections where students had identified effective learning strategies.

Khun's entry (Figure 3-8) is an example of a reflection that helped a student understand that the power of learning strategies goes beyond the English classroom. Students had been working on imaging as a strategy to appreciate the details an author uses to create meaning for the reader. Their journal entries were done in the form of a rough sketch (called sketch to

Reflections on Group

    I like the groups because they clear up a lot of problems for me, like unknown vocabulary words, hard dialouge and/or storylines, and which way to side on controversial things that happen in the book. Now I don't get as confused, and I get to see how other people stand on certain issues involving Huck, Jim, and the book in general.

Figure 3-6.

    I don't know about everyone else, but group discussion makes me feel more independent. It's better to have more freedom when reading a book. It doesn't add to the boredom, and it gives you time to reflect on what you read. You also understand it more because you can get other ideas. You're not just limited to your own.

Figure 3-7.

stretch) accompanied by a narrative that explained why the details were vivid to them. At one point in Khun's portfolio there were two sketches followed by reflection. When Janell questioned Khun further, she explained that she found she could apply this strategy while reading her history and biology assignments. Khun discovered that she could apply this strategy whenever she ran into difficulties.

REFLECTION ALLOWS LEARNERS TO CELEBRATE RISK TAKING AND INQUIRY

Constructing meaning is an interactive process that requires risk-taking because intellectual growth is supported by poor decisions as well as by good ones. Risk-taking might cause us to make mistakes, but by playing it safe learners can "short circuit" their opportunities to learn (Calkins 1986, 80). The fear of being wrong and therefore not taking risks have impeded most learners at one time or another, but through reflection they can see the valuable role that this factor plays in the learning process. When learners explore their natural curiosity through inquiry and then look back on it by using the portfolio as a strategy, achievements can be showcased (Valencia 1990, 338). Through the use of a portfolio, the interactions that supported learners in their development can be made public. A celebration such as this informs not only the learner, but also others who interact with the author of the portfolio.

One of the most dramatic illustrations of risk-taking we have seen is Angel's, who was placed in the Chapter I program upon his arrival from El Salvador. He realizes that by making mistakes he is creating opportunities for his literacy development. Figure 3-9 shows the introductory page of his portfolio. In the pages of Angel's portfolio, he shared stories about his family, his fears, and his dreams. Each successive piece showed evidence of hard work, careful revision, and risk-taking as he began to explore and create a process that helped him become comfortable with his second language.

On the final page of Hemal's portfolio, shown in Figure 3-10, he celebrated his growth by listing the changes he had noticed in his reading and writing. Thad listed the titles of the novels he had read during his first-semester English class. Then he inserted a simple, but honest, reflection that would definitely qualify as a risk for a freshman boy who was trying to achieve a delicate balance between academics, athletics, and popularity (see Figure 3-11).

Experimentation, approximation, and refinement are required whenever a learner attempts to learn something new (Crafton 1991, 15). Language-learning requires that we go beyond what we can do by trying ideas that hold possibilities for meaning and by celebrating our discoveries.

REFLECTION ALLOWS LEARNERS TO SET GOALS FOR FUTURE EXPERIENCES

Learning is never complete; one experience is connected to the next. When learners look back at the interactions that changed them, the person they need to become can be put into personal perspective. As a learning strategy,

Sketch to Stretch

My first sketch from <u>Tuck Everlasting</u> isn't as detailed as "Antaeus." The first picture was my first experience in using sketch to stretch to further understand a story. The second time around, I learned to spill my ideas better on paper and form a picture of each scene as I went. Now, I have learned to draw in my mind instead of physically on paper. I usually use the same method when I'm trying to understand information in other classes.

Figure 3-8.

the portfolio becomes a part of the curriculum that informs interpretative evaluation, which in turn informs curriculum (Goodman 1989, 9). The answer(s) to the question, "What needs to be done next?" can only be determined when individual strengths, weaknesses, needs, and questions are brought to the conscious level of both student and teacher.

Lisa chose to organize her portfolio around the theme "Following the Footsteps of My Growth." The reflection pages between artifacts were

This Portfolio have that I learned in this year, for me was dificult learn, because when I came to this class I didn't speak inglish well and this problem was the frist barrier what I have to defeat.

In the portfolio I write some stories about me, my parents, my country and expiernces what happened. Write is dificult but is good talk about of you and expiernces what you was live.

I don't write well but I learn of my mistakes and the opinions of my teachers and friends. Like result I get this........

Figure 3-9.

Figure 3-10.

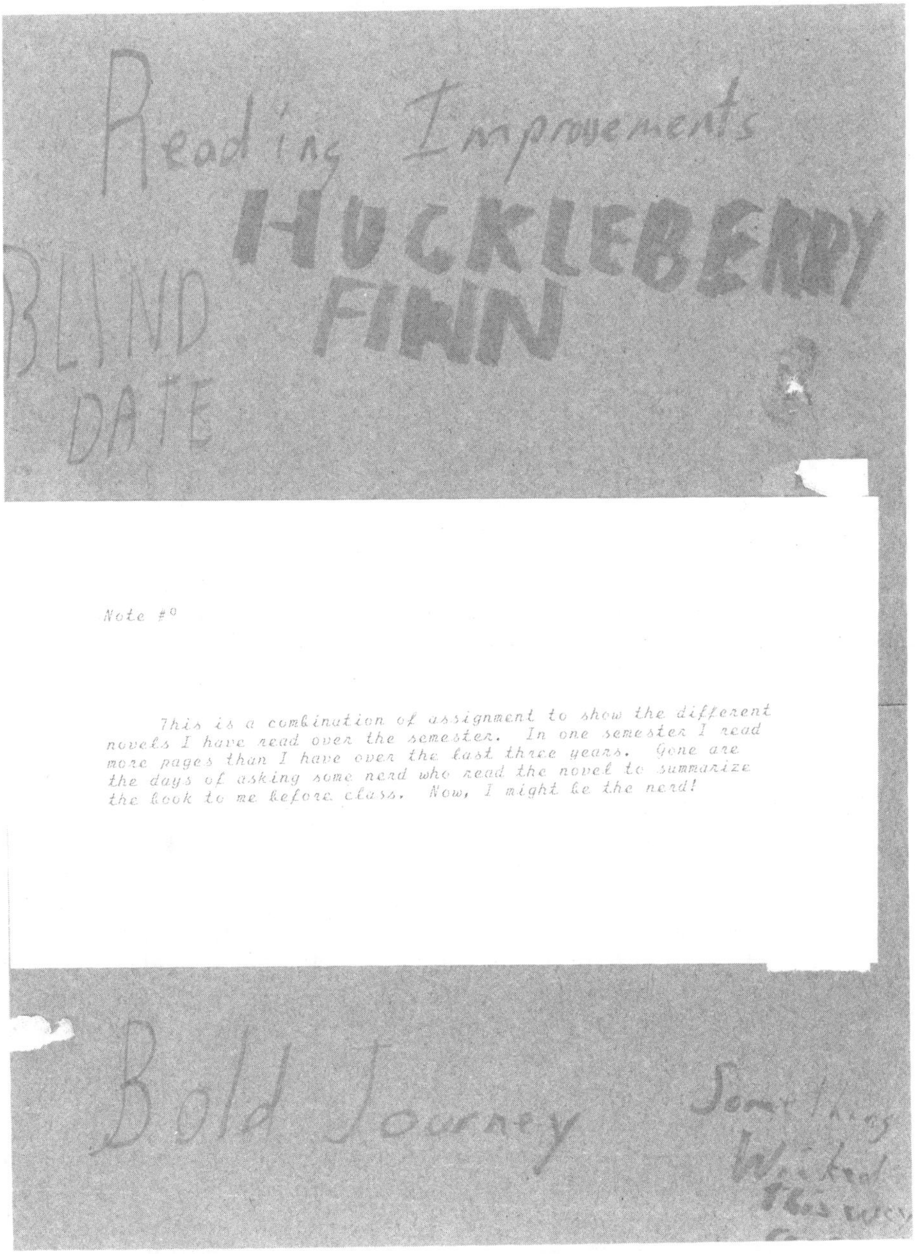
Reading Improvements
HUCKLEBERRY FINN
BLIND DATE
Note #9
This is a combination of assignment to show the different novels I have read over the semester. In one semester I read more pages than I have over the last three years. Gone are the days of asking some nerd who read the novel to summarize the book to me before class. Now, I might be the nerd!
Bold Journey

Figure 3-11.

decorated with colorful footprints. The following example, shown in Figure 3-12, is the closing reflection in her portfolio where she examines her strengths, the areas she perceives as weaknesses, and sets goals for the upcoming semester.

REFLECTION ALLOWS LEARNERS TO SEE CHANGES AND DEVELOPMENT OVER TIME

We have all experienced times when we are so closely tied to a project that we are no longer objective about its quality. We become overly critical of our efforts and feel that we are not making any progress. We become so bogged down with the project that we actually feel we are getting worse rather than better. No amount of reassurance can convince us that these feelings are a natural part of the learning process—that when we reach this level of discomfort with our work, we might actually be experimenting with techniques that will make our work even stronger than when we seemed to be "on a roll."

This was true of Lisa during the spring of her senior year. She was frustrated with what seemed like her inability to correctly punctuate her work. She could not understand why suddenly she and Mrs. Cleland were setting punctuation goals during their conferences. She had not set punctuation goals since she was a sophomore. As she so aptly stated it, "Just my luck—just as I'm getting ready to graduate, I begin to forget what I thought I knew." Janell suggested that Lisa collect a sampling of work from earlier semesters and examine why this goal was re-occurring.

Lisa's reflection provided the support she needed. Of course she was experiencing new problems. She was using complex sentences filled with descriptive phrases and dependent clauses. Her earlier work revealed only simple sentences with an occasional introductory word, series, or compound sentence. Janell was also able to point out that the complex punctuation questions Lisa was now asking would cause even the most proficient writer to consult a reference book. By examining her previous work and reflecting on her changes, Lisa could celebrate her growth and see the concrete evidence that she needed to illustrate that she was indeed moving forward and working at a higher level, not regressing to a prior stage of her writing development.

Probably the most dramatic example of this need for reassurance occurs in May with our senior Chapter I students. Many of them have been with us for two years and have become accustomed to an environment where risk-taking is encouraged and celebrated. They view the classroom as a haven for their experimentation with reading and writing, but as their high school career draws to a close, they begin to experience doubts about their ability to succeed outside that haven. By returning to previous work as far back as their freshman year, they are able to validate their growth and alleviate their

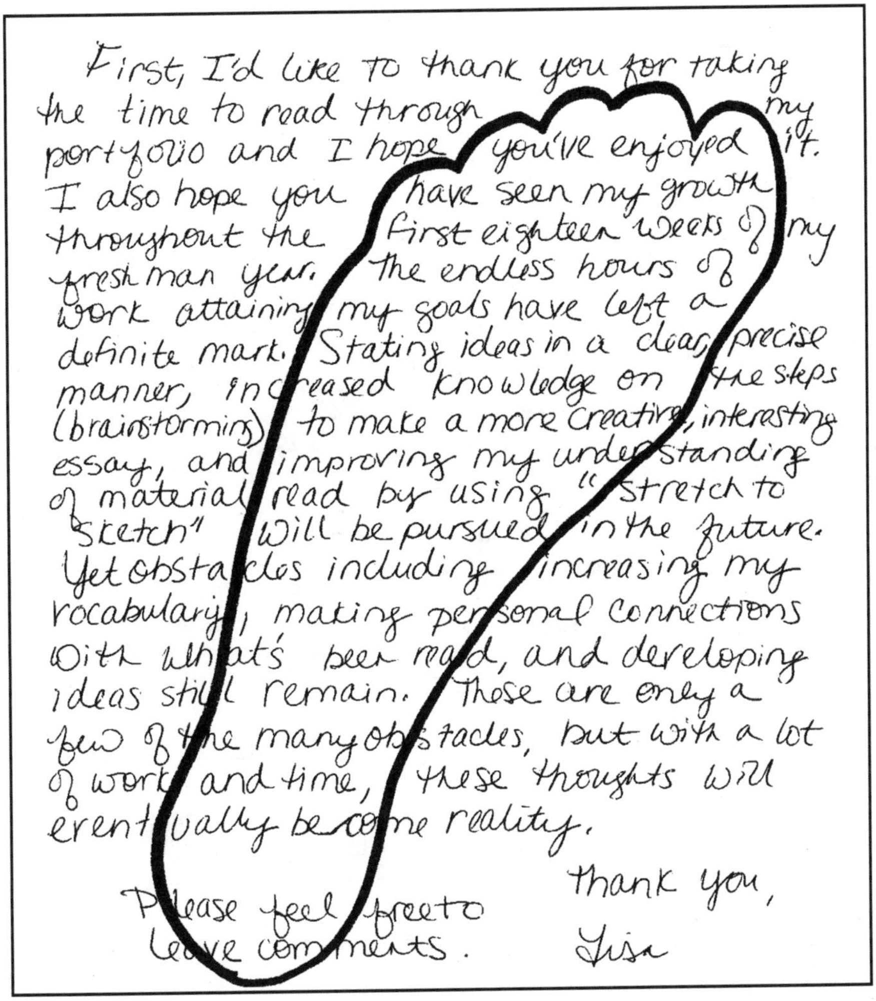

First, I'd like to thank you for taking the time to read through my portfolio and I hope you've enjoyed it. I also hope you have seen my growth throughout the first eighteen weeks of my freshman year. The endless hours of work attaining my goals have left a definite mark. Stating ideas in a clear, precise manner, increased knowledge on the steps (brainstorming) to make a more creative, interesting essay, and improving my understanding of material read by using "stretch to sketch" will be pursued in the future. Yet obstacles including increasing my vocabulary, making personal connections with what's been read, and developing ideas still remain. These are only a few of the many obstacles, but with a lot of work and time, these thoughts will eventually become reality.

Please feel free to leave comments.

thank you,

Lisa

Figure 3-12.

fears. Many of them chose to begin their final portfolio with a piece from September of their freshman year, and some add pictures of themselves to further emphasize their growth. The change is so dramatic that it provides the confidence boost they need to reassure them they are ready for "life after high school."

Reflection over time can provide support that we all periodically need when it seems we have been in the same place for an extended period of time. This use of reflection can serve as our own personal pep rally. It can shout, "Look what you've been able to accomplish" just at a time when we need it the most. It can provide the concrete evidence we need as we begin to doubt the verbal reassurances from our peers as token attempts to boost our confidence. It is one thing to be told that we are improving, but it is an entirely different matter when we can view the changes ourselves.

By substituting the word reflection for the word portfolio, Jason helps us understand that portfolios can become vehicles for sharing reflections with an audience that includes oneself.

> I like to do portfolios because in most classes the teachers say, "Your making a lot of progress," but you never see the progress yourself. I think the portfolio is more for your benefit because you can see yourself growing and changing as a reader and a writer, and when I see the change myself it is much more rewarding than when a teacher tells me I am changing.
>
> Jason

Portfolios can open a window into the students' minds creating a means for the teacher, students, and administration to understand the educational process at the level of the individual learner (Paulson, Paulson and Meyer 1991, 61).

And, of course, by opening that window, we also open a Pandora's box of new questions:

- As teachers, how can we use the information from a student's reflections to help that student?
- How can students learn to use the information from reflections to set future goals and work toward those goals?
- What are some reflective strategies we can implement in the classroom on a weekly or monthly basis?
- How do the categories discussed in this chapter impact instruction?
- What other categories might emerge as we experiment with portfolios and reflection?

DO YOU HAVE a drawer in your house filled to overflowing with photos you have collected over the years? If you are like us, you have good intentions and mean to put these pictures into a photo album, but they pile up faster than you can organize them. When we finally get around to the monumental task of sorting and making some sense of the mess, there always seems to be that one stack of pictures for which we can't remember the people, places and/or events. There are usually just as many pictures we stare at longer than the rest or return to because they bring a smile to our faces. If we take a moment to reflect, those are probably the pictures in which the people, places and/or events changed us in some way.

If we were telling our autobiographies or even focusing on one specific year, we would pick and choose experiences to relate rather than include every detail. That's the difference between a good biography that keeps the reader anxiously turning the pages and the one that falls to the bedroom floor because the reader can't get through the tedious details. Those life experiences that are different from the rest, just as the special photos in the above example, are probably related to the people, places, and/or events that have had a personal effect on us.

By correlating the photo album and the autobiography to the learning folders of our students, we were able to see that our students should choose the artifacts from their learning experiences that changed them in some way. As teachers, our choosing items to place in the portfolio for the students made no more sense than taking our picture drawer to a friend and asking that person to organize our pictures in an album for us. If the friend included every picture and we tried to tell the significance that each one had on us, we would create that tedious biography that causes more frustration than learning for both writers and readers. Our friend might be able to pick and choose the photos that are more memorable than others from what they know of our lives, but the unconscious reasons for significance are not always discovered until a personal reflection determines the underlying meaning. As teachers, we should have a level of understanding about the importance of learning experiences to the students in our classes; however, only the students have the capacity to make personal meaning through their choices.

Having made these connections, our students were finally given the ownership they rightfully deserved in choosing what to display in their portfolios. When they began to own the process, we started to see artifacts ranging from a Burger King napkin on which a student had recorded an idea for a piece of writing while eating a late night snack, to a midterm report that had been hidden from parents under a bed but put to good use for a rough draft when an inspiration came but no paper was available, to a piece of yarn that symbolized the theme of a school speech written and given by that student. When we saw and read about the meanings these objects held, we realized our vision of learning was limited to the classroom experiences we had observed or heard about. However, when learners are making connections to experiences outside the classroom (as they should be), a teacher's agenda or a district's purpose can hamper learning if students are not the sole authors of their portfolios. As a learning strategy, the difference between students choosing their own artifacts and someone else determining what should be displayed is the difference between students writing their autobiography and having someone else write a student's biography. The author of the autobiography presents facts and learns from personal interpretations and insights, whereas the author of the biography presents facts and guesses at possible interpretations.

Typically, when we introduce portfolios to students, we come together as a class to generate a list of the artifacts they might choose to put into their portfolios. This discussion might begin by having students look through their folders. We also ask our students if there are some items in their folders that are personally more important than others. Learners have a variety of reasons to explain the importance of artifacts, but, somehow, they are always linked to meaningfulness. When Carol's son, Ryan, put together a portfolio at the end of his year in kindergarten, he determined the artifacts for his portfolio by choosing items he didn't want to throw away. Although Ryan may not have understood the concept of meaningful artifacts related to his learning experiences in the same way as our high school students do, he was able to state his reasons for keeping the pictures, stories, notes, and certificates he chose.

The list of possible items to include in the portfolio varies because it is reflective of the types of learning experiences with which students have been involved. Writing on newsprint the lists generated by students and displaying them in the classroom throughout the portfolio process has been a helpful reminder to students when they are making their choices. These lists, shown in Figure 4-1, can also be reflective tools for teachers as they look back on the meaningful strategies that students used to support their learning and the highlights of their learning experiences over a period of time.

As we stated previously, we realize that the types of artifacts available when students open their folders are representative of each individual's learning environment. Five years ago, if someone had suggested that our students display an understanding of their learning in the classes we taught by gathering artifacts and reflecting on their changes, their portfolios would have consisted of workbook pages, dittos, answers to questions from the end of chapters or stories, and tests. Their reflections on learning would have analyzed how successfully they could memorize, fill in blanks, and take a test. We have come a long way in the past five years and we felt it might be helpful to share the types of artifacts our students choose most frequently and share the reasons for their choices.

Figure 4-1.

ARTIFACTS THAT REPRESENT STRATEGIES

Journal Entries

Responding in writing to literature that has been read is a strategy students can use to reflect on their thoughts from reading and create new meanings for themselves. Journal entries might represent a meaningful piece of literature, the discovery of a new process, the emergence of a more committed reader, and a significant change in the thoughts of a reader before, during, and/or after reading. The response to the literature might be written in a notebook, on a scrap of paper, or on blank pages at the end of the book or chapter.

Mike chose one of his journal entries in response to *The Crazy Horse Electric Game* for his portfolio because it represented one of his favorite novels. When he compared this entry—shown in Figure 4-2—to previous ones, Mike was able to see that he was no longer just passing his eyes over the words, but was now actively involved in the process and using strategies to support his understanding.

Dear Mrs. Porter,

I understand that Willie is good at sports, but my question is why is he such a god in that town? I like how Johnny plays catcher that is the proper way to play the game. Wow! I didn't notice that it is football season now until Shawn told me.

Mike

Figure 4-2.

Bookmarks

Used in the same way and for the same purposes as journal entries, bookmarks only differ in size of the paper and the place where they are kept. We cut 8-1/2" by 11" sheets of paper lengthwise and students place a number of them in their books both to mark their place when they finished reading and to respond to literature during and after reading.

Ann chose to include her bookmarks—see Figure 4-3—from *The Adventures of Huckleberry Finn* by Mark Twain in a section of her portfolio where she highlighted the reading strategies that she found most effective.

Color-Coded Responses to Literature

Identifying the processes students use to create meaning can be difficult. By having students share and analyze their journal entries and bookmarks, they can determine some of the process strategies that support their understanding of the written word. Our students have found it easier to bring these to a more conscious level by color-coding their written responses to reading. Students can set goals for themselves as readers based upon this type of analysis because they are able to see the strategies they're using while constructing their personal meaning of the text. If the strategies are shared with partners or larger groups, students can apply strategies they, perhaps, hadn't previously considered.

Ann used her *Huckleberry Finn* bookmarks to examine the different ways she responded to the text to help her create her personal meaning. By highlighting her responses using a color-code system, as shown in Figure 4-4, she found that she tended to rely on personal connections, personal opinions,

Chapters 1-5

I was the same kind-of kid Tom Sawyer is, always getting my way, exaggerating things a little here, and a little there. I was more the leader than the follower.

I think Tom + Huck make perfect friends, one who's the most gullible thing, and the other who always gets his way.

I really like the way the author makes you feel, as if you know Tom + Huck by the end of Chapter 2! you get a real clear picture of their personalities.

I think Jim is going to play a big part in whatever huge scheme Tom + Huck try to pull off next.

Chapters 6-10

I really liked the very first paragraph in chapter 6. many times there has been something I didn't want to do, but as soon as my parents told me I couldn't do it, I couldn't wait until I could do it.

I think Mark Twain has a real good grasp on childrens reactions, no matter their age, sex, or the time period.

I didn't understand the mans joke about the short days. what is quick silver? On page 48 injun is mentioned again, what is that?

I really miss Tom. within a few chapters, Twain made me really start to like him.

Figure 4-3.

and predictions. One goal she set for herself was to ask more authentic questions, like the ones she had seen on other class members' bookmarks on days we shared and analyzed our responses as a group.

Written Conversation

As this title implies, two or more people are engaged in "talk" on paper. In our classrooms, we use this strategy as a way for students to respond to the

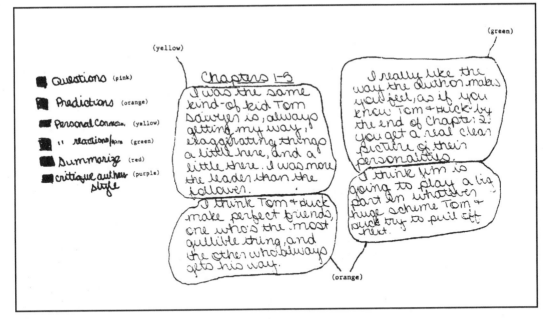

Figure 4-4.

literature they have read in ways similar to journal entries. The sharing of ideas directly with another reader and writer often yields genuine questions for which immediate responses might be gained (Gilles et al. 1988, 35). In Figure 4-5, Lauren explains the written conversations she included in her portfolio by first explaining the strategy.

After seeing many of the written conversations that their moms were reading from their students, Carol's daughter, Michelle, and Janell's son, Justin, decided they didn't want to be left out of something that looked like fun. Justin had a book report due in his sixth grade language-arts class and Michelle (an eighth grader) agreed to be his partner. They chose *Bridge to Terabithia*, by Katherine Patterson. Michelle's first note (see Figure 4-6) set the parameters for their reading, and Justin responded by giving his reading suggestions, shown in Figure 4-7.

Their written conversation moved beyond asking each other questions, making predictions, and sharing likes and dislikes as they began to share personal concerns and interests. Carol noticed that Michelle, who seldom read for pleasure, expressed a new commitment to reading when she had an authentic audience (see Figure 4-8). Janell was thrilled to watch her reluctant writer fill pages as he corresponded with Michelle, a sample of which is shown in Figure 4-9.

In this pocket is something called written conversation. It is not actually a type of bookmark because it is between two people, but I am comparing it with the types of bookmarks. First of all, written conversation is just what it sounds like. You write your reaction to something read in class in a note form to someone, and then they write back, adding some of their reactions, answering some of your questions, and asking a few of their own.

Figure 4-5.

Walking Journal

Many times we have students who want to read a book, but do not have a partner for discussion. The walking journal travels from one class to another and is the vehicle for written conversations between partners who do not share the same class period and/or teacher.

Wendy and Adam's written conversation, shown in Figures 4-10 and 4-11, provides a glimpse of how they set the groundwork for their shared discussion. Adam, who was extremely shy, seldom shared any response in class and found it difficult to finish a novel. He included a copy of this conversation in his portfolio with a reflection that revealed how the nonthreatening nature of this strategy allowed him to take risks that even surprised him.

Sketch to Stretch

This strategy is used in our classrooms as an alternative form of communication about literature that has been read. Just as the journal entry is a response to reading, sketching an interpretation has provided many of our students with their first experience in imaging. Being able to see multiple (and acceptable) interpretations of the same text has also been valuable to students previously afraid to take risks (Harste, Short, and Burke 353).

The following sketches in Figure 4-12 accompanied Khun's reflection from Chapter 3. She placed her first attempt at this strategy beside her most recent example to highlight her growth in imaging.

A variation of sketch to stretch occurs when students ask the members of their authors' circle to sketch as a means of providing feedback on details they have used in their writing.

Lynn was uncertain if the details in a descriptive essay she was writing were creating the pictures in her readers' minds that she intended. She asked her authors' circle to listen to her piece and then sketch what was most vivid to them. The resulting pictures, shown in Figure 4-13, allowed Lynn to analyze similarities and omissions to determine her next revisions. She included the sketches in her portfolio to show a step she added to her writing process that worked effectively for her.

Dear Justin,

Hi how are you? How is basketball? I had a game yesterday and we lost. Well when do you want to start reading Bridge to Terabithia? Do you want to write letters every night? If we read one chapter a night we could be done in thirteen nights and then have 13 letters. Then our moms could exchange the letters and give them to us. I can start reading whenever you want to.

From,
Michelle

WBS

P.S Can you believe there is going to be a war!

Figure 4-6.

Dear Michelle,

My mom brought the note home after school so I decided to write back. I'm ready to start the book over the weekend. How about we read three chapters and then right back on Monday? I'm looking forward to reading this book. One of my friends just did this book for an oral book report. It sounded like a great book!

Justin

Figure 4-7.

Dear Justin,

YO! Did you like chapter five? I did. That was pretty good how Jesse and Leslie wrote the letter to Janice. Do you think that Jesse and Leslie will get caught doing more of this stuff like writing letters and sneaking them around. I don't think that the book is boring anymore because now there is more excitement. Can you believe that there is war !! (not good though) Who do you think is going to win? I think U.S. A is because there is more people on all side. I have been watching the news ever since the war started. Oh for X-mas we got Festers Quest, Goonies #, and Legacy Of The Wizard. Tyler forgot Mega Man II over here we only have one guy to beat then Dr. Whilies stage (or however you spell it). Well I better go and get to bed! So chapter 8 and letter due on Friday and three chapters over the weekend and a letter on the three chapters due on monday? Chow

From,
Michelle

P.S.
Thanks for the cards what do you like or want?

mr. Jim
and

Purple
People
eater

P.P.S
If you have any questions call.

Figure 4-8.

Dear Michelle,

Hi! What's up! This was a real short chapter. I loved the way they set Janice Avery up and she had to walk all the way home. Don't you think May Belle diserved to get her Twinkies stolen? She said ~~Yum~~ she had Twinkies so long that the hole bus heard her. That was a good stall by Leslie to get the teacher to go look at a birds nest while he found her desk. I think Janice Avery is even worse than Gary Fulcher. What do you think? Before I even heard what she was like I pictured a big fat mean bully always picking on little kids for laughs. On a 1-10 What would you give this book so far. Well I

have to go. Say hi to Ryan for me.

Justin

P. S.
Do You get
AIR JORDAN
FLIGT CLUB
MAGAZINE?

(Write back
soon)   (Please answer)

Figure 4-9.

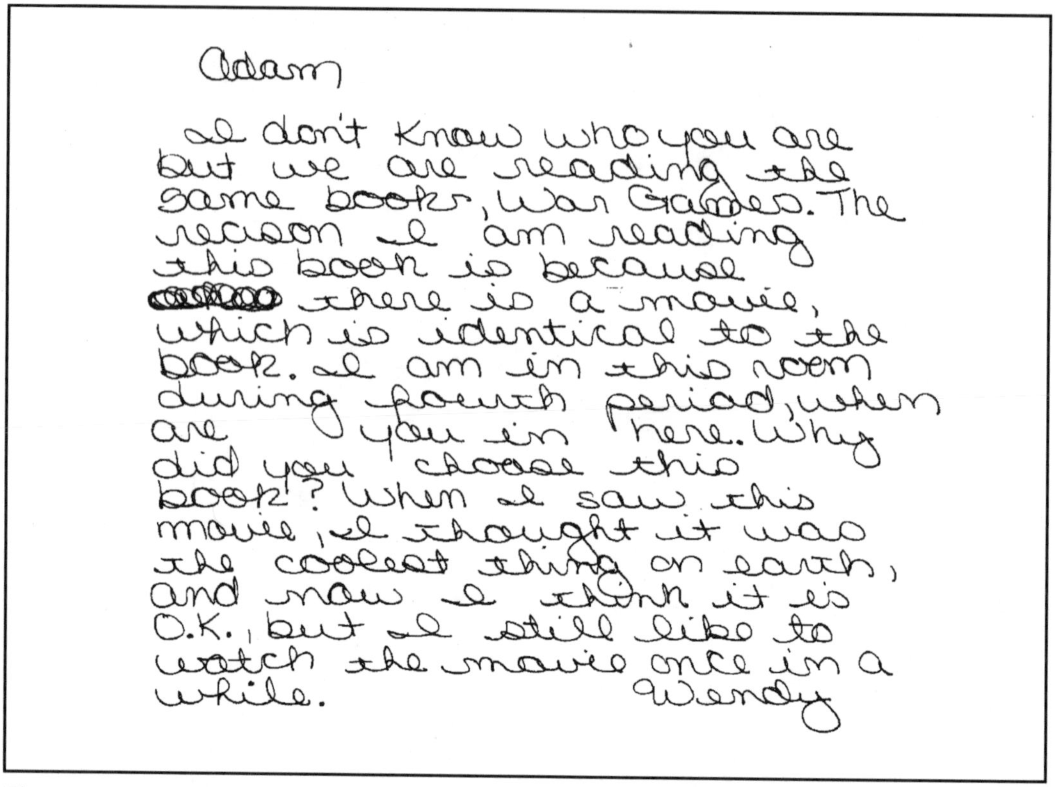

Adam

I don't know who you are but we are reading the same book, War Games. The reason I am reading this book is because ~~there~~ there is a movie, which is identical to the book. I am in this room during fourth period, when are you in here. Why did you choose this book? When I saw this movie, I thought it was the coolest thing on earth, and now I think it is O.K., but I still like to watch the movie once in a while.

Wendy

Figure 4-10.

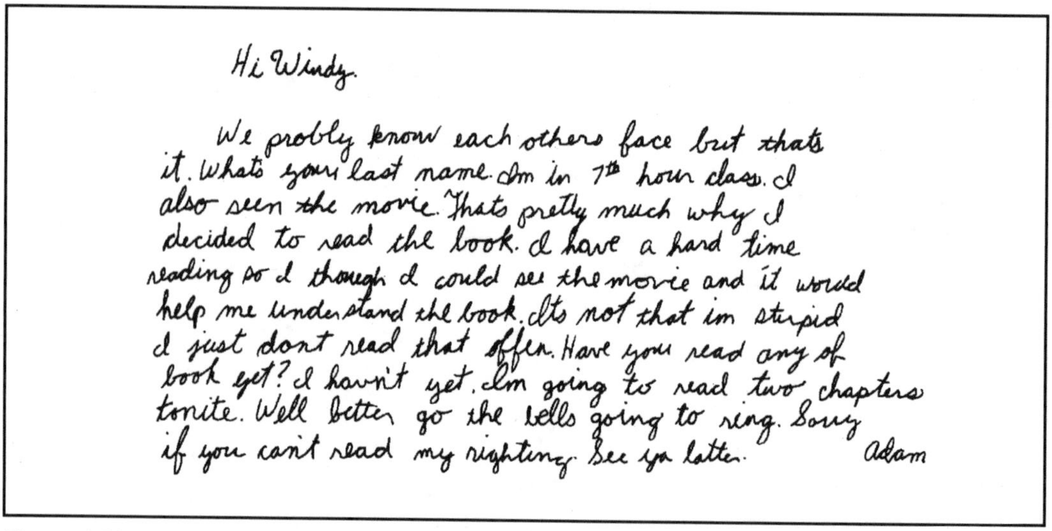

Hi Windy.

We probly know each others face but thats it. Whats your last name. Im in 7th hour class. I also seen the movie. Thats pretty much why I decided to read the book. I have a hard time reading so I though I could see the movie and it would help me understand the book. Its not that im stupid I just dont read that offen. Have you read any of book yet? I havn't yet. Im going to read two chapters tonite. Well better go the bells going to ring. Sorry if you cant read my righting. See ya later.

Adam

Figure 4-11.

Figure 4-12.

Figure 4-13.

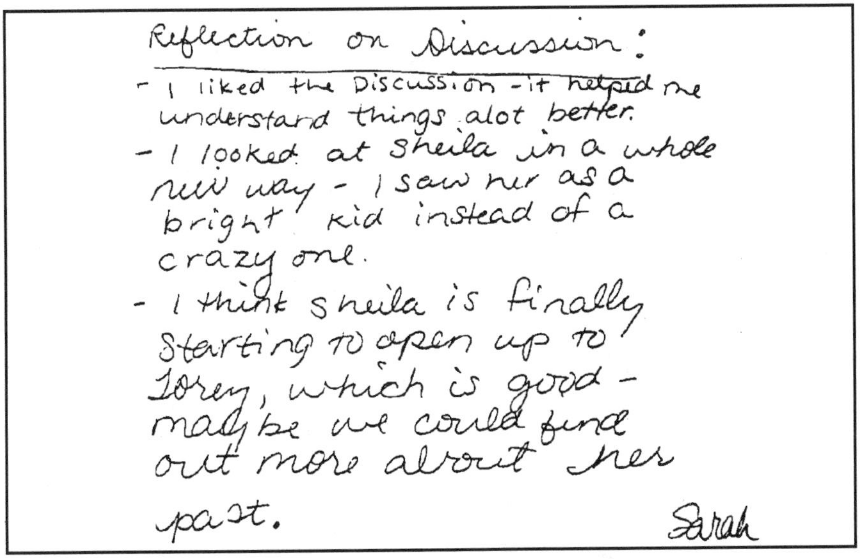

Reflection on Discussion:
- I liked the Discussion - it helped me understand things alot better.
- I looked at Sheila in a whole new way - I saw her as a bright kid instead of a crazy one.
- I think Sheila is finally starting to open up to Torey, which is good - maybe we could find out more about her past.
                                        Sarah

Figure 4-14.

Reflections on Discussion

As literature discussions draw to a close, students write about questions answered, revisions and extensions of original ideas, differences in interpretation among group members, and new ideas. Figure 4-14 shows how students might also analyze their changing role in using discussion as a learning strategy.

Authors' Circle Comments

When students choose a rough-draft piece of writing to take to final draft, sharing at authors' circle is a strategy in which they receive feedback for revisions. The author reads the draft to the other members of the group, which can vary in size from a single partner to the entire class. When the reading is completed, each group member asks the author questions to help him/her with revisions. Responses are in the form of questions and focus on content (Harste, Short, and Burke 20). Our students prefer writing their responses on slips of paper that are passed to the author after everyone has shared their comments. When students' responses include a praise statement, this becomes a helpful tool to writers who are apprehensive about sharing and helps the listener focus on qualities of good writing.

After reading a piece of her writing to one of her classes, Carol received the authors' circle comments shown in Figure 4-15. They provided her with questions that helped her revise the content of her piece; they also provided praise statements that highlighted her strengths.

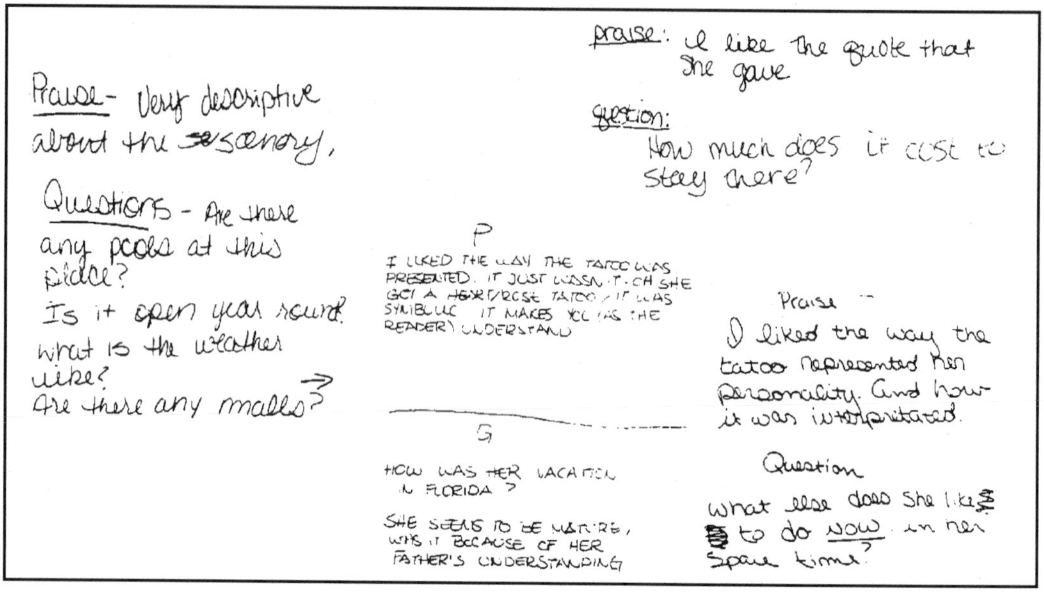
Praise- Very descriptive about the scenery,

Questions - Are there any pools at this place?
Is it open year round?
what is the weather like?
Are there any malls?

P
I LIKED THE WAY THE TATOO WAS PRESENTED. IT JUST WASN'T THAT SHE GOT A HEART/ROSE TATOO, IT WAS SYMBOLIC. IT MAKES YOU (AS THE READER) UNDERSTAND

Q
HOW WAS HER VACATION IN FLORIDA?

SHE SEEMS TO BE MATURE, WAS IT BECAUSE OF HER FATHER'S UNDERSTANDING

praise: I like the quote that she gave

question:
How much does it cost to stay there?

Praise —
I liked the way the tatoo represented her personality. And how it was interpretated.

Question
what else does she like to do now in her spare time?

Figure 4-15.

Reflections on Writing Process

Similar to reflections on literature discussions, taking time to step back from the writing itself to determine the thought processes, decisions, revisions, difficulties, discoveries, and strategies used provide the learner with directions and alternatives for future experiences.

It is evident from Deirdre's reflection on her writing process, shown in Figure 4-16, that authors' circle is a strategy for revision that has and will continue to provide her with support. She has discovered that her strategy is applicable to other learning situations beyond her English classroom.

In-Process Photographs

Photographs taken while students use various strategies can depict portions of the learning process that can't be displayed in other ways. Students might also be photographed when they are taking a risk, becoming more personally involved in the learning, or investigating questions or ideas. After our students put together their first portfolios they realized the need to capture meaningful learning experiences that are not documented in writing or by means of some other type of artifact. Now they use the class camera to take pictures, making sure they list on a photograph sheet the person taking the shot and the reason for taking it. Photographs are placed in their learning folders. Kate, Katy,

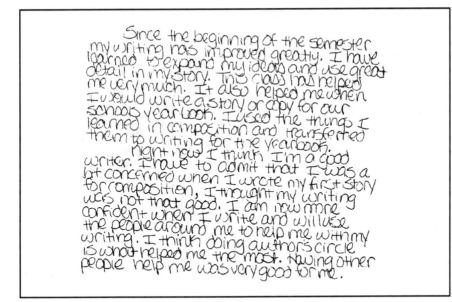

Since the beginning of the semester my writing has improved greatly. I have learned to expand my ideas and use great detail in my story. This class has helped me very much. It also helped me when I would write a story or copy for our schools yearbook. I used the things I learned in composition and transferred them to writing for the yearbook.
Right now I think I'm a good writer. I have to admit that I was a bit concerned when I wrote my first story for composition, I thought my writing was not that good. I am now more confident when I write and will use the people around me to help me with my writing. I think doing authors circle is what helped me the most. Having other people help me was very good for me.

Figure 4-16.

Sarah, and Tim investigated the qualities of an effective personal narrative by reading sample student essays. Photograph 4-1 shows them listing their discoveries on newsprint to share with classmates and then to post in the classroom as a reminder when they write their own narratives. Jorge chose the picture shown in Photograph 4-2 for his portfolio as an example of a risk he took when he shared a personal experience story with his classmates. Linda and Tim's total involvement in their learning was uncharacteristic of their participation just a few months earlier. We felt the need to capture these moments for them, shown in Photographs 4-3 and 4-4. Authors' circle, pictured in Photograph 4-5, was a strategy that provided Glenn with the feedback he needed to support his revision process. Photograph 4-6 shows Yada, who preferred to use a typewriter to compose her bookmarks with her novel at her side.

ARTIFACTS THAT REPRESENT LEARNING HIGHLIGHTS

Book Covers

Photocopies of book covers can represent books that students associate with memorable learning experiences.

Yada chose to include a photocopy of each novel she read during the semester, and she devised her own rating system. Her first and last pages

Photograph 4-1.

Photograph 4-2.

Photograph 4-3.

Photograph 4-4.

Photograph 4-5.

Photograph 4-6.

are shared here and shown in Figures 4-17 and 4-18. There were eight other novels shown in her actual portfolio for a total of twelve novels in eighteen weeks. The brief reflection on the last page of her portfolio reveals how proud Yada is of this accomplishment.

First Through Final Drafts

By displaying a piece of writing from its inception to publication, students are able to celebrate their achievements and analyze their development, decisionmaking, and revision process.

Cecilia was able to trace her favorite piece back to a bookmark from *All I Ever Needed to Know I Learned in Kindergarten*, by Robert Fulghum. She extended the bookmark into a rough draft (see Figure 4-19) that she presented to our authors' circle. Her portfolio also included the comment from authors' circle that provided her with the most help. These were followed by two more drafts and a picture of her great-grandparents, shown in Figure 4-20. Cecilia was able to determine that her best ideas seem to come from her favorite reading.

My Heroes

A hero in my eyes isn't someone who saves another person's life. It can be someone who loves and does something about what's going on in life. Someone who tries to help you or someone else get through difficult times by doing something instead of just talking about it.

My heroes are two people even though in my eyes they are one. They passed away in 1988 and 1989. They were so close that they died within 3 months of each other because my great-grandma couldn't live without my great-grandpa even though she was very healthy. As you might have figured out they are my great-grandparents.

They are my heroes because of the kind of life that they lived. They lived in Mexico on a ranch. Even though they were my dad's grandparents, he and all of his cousins called them Mom and Dad. They raised them, so that's why they called them Mom and Dad. They did anything and everything possible to have their children, grandchildren, and great-grandchildren live a happy life as well as become educated because they believed that you couldn't get somewhere in life without education. They even sold some of their property and their animals to make sure that everyone had at least the basics they needed and could go further if they wanted to go to school. Even into my generation they would help.

My most memorable time with them was when I was twelve years old and our whole family went down to Mexico. We surprised them by having an anniversary party for them with the whole family. About 350 people showed up, and we all had a good time. They made sure they danced with each and every one of us, which was something they hadn't done since they were in their early 20's and now they were in their late 80's. To please everyone they stayed until the party ended.

1 = Drop the Book
2 = Kinda dumb
3 = An O.K reading
4 = It's good
5 = A very good book
6 = The best book ever

PLAY TO WIN
GARY JUST WANTS TO WIN AGAIN

Winning

These are all of the books that I have read for this school year. They are in the order in which I read them. I also rated each book. The key is at the top.

Figure 4-17.

Figure 4-18.

My Hero

My heroes are my great-grandparents because of the kind of people that they were. They raised my dad, his brothers and sisters and cousins. They would sell land or anything needed to be sold so you could go to school and buy them the basics needed. If it was your birthday or something they'd ask you what your favorite food was and what you wanted as a gift and they'd try to get it for you as well as making your favorite food. They loved each-other til the day they died. If it wasn't for them my family would be scattered everywhere and they would never had achieved the things they did.

Figure 4-19.

They helped people who weren't blood-related and would treat them as if they were family. Everyone respected them from young to old. In return they respected you. In the town they were recognized all the time because they always contributed money or animals to the schools for charity to pay the tuition of students who couldn't afford to pay. They always bought the things that the children would sell to raise tuition money as well as making others buy the things.

The main thing about them was that they would treat you as an adult even if you were a little kid and they wouldn't criticize you or your thoughts. They would tell you their thoughts and would just hope you followed them but wouldn't say anything if you didn't. The main reason that they are my heroes is because of the people that they were and the person they made me.

Nonfiction

The significance of information found in newspapers, magazines, or other non-fiction sources might include ideas for writing, topics for debate, answers to areas of inquiry, and connections between literature and modern day experiences.

Jason's area of interest and expertise is cooking and it was cookbooks that hooked him to do his best reading and writing, so Carol wasn't surprised to see the following entries (Figure 4-21) in his portfolio. (To fully appreciate Jason's growth over the two years he was in our program, return to his first bookmarks from *Don't Look Behind You*, by Lois Duncan, in Chapter 2.)

Celebrations

As the culminating activity for personal inquiry, students celebrate their learning by making a personal interpretation to the class or another appropriate audience (Harste, Short, and Burke 92). Just as this book is a celebration of our personal inquiries in portfolios, students often use writing as a format for interpretation, too. Others have created videos, skits, board games, posters, mobiles, puppet shows, and newspapers. The artifacts or photographs of celebrations are often memorable experiences shared in the portfolio.

Carey, Tracy, and Darcey created puppets for each of the characters from the *Sword and the Stone* in *The Once and Future King*, by T. H. White. They rewrote their favorite scene as a play and presented it to the class. They included their script and photographs of their puppets in their portfolio, shown in Figure 4-22.

Audiotapes

Students might include an audiotape in their portfolio to represent a strategy for creating a rough-draft piece of writing, an editing device that has been effective for them, a song that was significant to their learning, their changes in risk-taking during group discussions, or a speech that they gave.

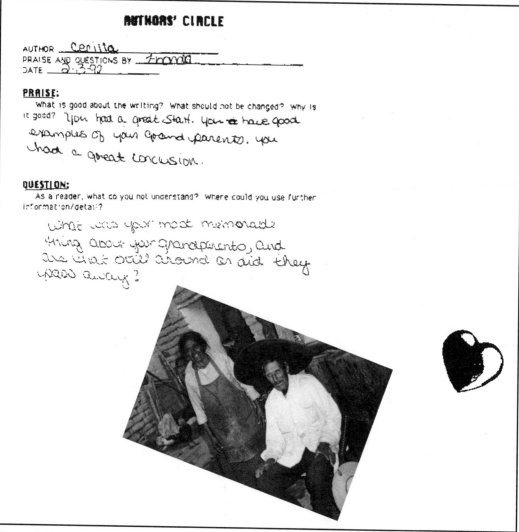

AUTHORS' CIRCLE

AUTHOR _Cecilia_

PRAISE AND QUESTIONS BY _Amanda_

DATE _2-3-92_

PRAISE:

What is good about the writing? What should not be changed? Why is it good? You had a great start. You have good examples of your grandparents. You had a great conclusion.

QUESTION:

As a reader, what do you not understand? Where could you use further information/detail?

What was your most memorable thing about your grandparents, and are that still around or did they pass away?

Figure 4-20.

Photographs

Many learning experiences are too large to display in the book-style format that our students currently use for their portfolios or there might have been a moment in time that couldn't be documented except in a photograph.

Rob's entry and accompanying photograph shown in Figure 4-23 need little explanation in order to understand why he included this experience in his portfolio:

"One of the great things that happened to me is that I got to share Halloween with others. When my classmates and I went off to a nearby school and told a ghost story that we had written to the little kids—that was the best! The reaction on their faces when they saw us said it all. Here is a picture of me with the little kids."

Art Work

Sketches, paintings, doodles, etc. may have been the inspiration or rough draft for a piece of writing, an interpretation of literature, or a connection between one communication system and another.

When Kelly read *Don't Look Behind You,* by Lois Duncan, he was able to create an image of the main character, April. Because his image was so strong, he decided to draw his own version of what he believed to be a better book cover, shown in Figure 4-24. Kelly also chose to sketch a hand coming from behind April rather than the character looking in the rearview mirror of her car since he believed this was a better representation of the suspense the author had created throughout the book.

Letters

Copies of letters written to or received from others may represent memorable learning experiences.

Lisa evolved into a reader when she discovered Chris Crutcher's books. Over a period of two years , Lisa not only read his books several times, but she also recommended them to classmates, friends, teachers . . . anyone she determined in need of a book (particularly reluctant readers as she had once been). When she was ready to move on to other authors and books, she wrote a letter to the author. Even though Lisa received her response from Chris Crutcher during the summer, it was a highlight in Lisa's portfolio during the following school year.

> Mundelein High School
> 1350 W. Hawley
> Mundelein, Il 60060

Dear Mr. Chris Crutcher,

My name is Lisa Salazar. I'm a junior at Mundelein High School in Illinois. I have just finished reading your book *The Crazy Horse Electric Game*, and I had all ready read your first book *Running Loose* last year. I enjoyed both books very much. I'm in a class called Chapter I Reading/Writing Lab. We were required to read *The Crazy Horse Electric Game*. When I heard that it was one of your books, I was glad because with the other book of yours I finished it in two days. For me that's good because I'm a slow reader, and for that I take a reading class.

The title of a cookbook is unimportant to me because it is just a collection of many different recipes and I don't start at the beginning and read to the end, I tend to go through it and find recipes that are interesting and unusual to make.

I made bookmarks for those recipes that I liked and thought about making. I rated each recipe for difficulty, description in how to make it, price, and the amount of time to make them.

One that interested me was a deep dish apple pie which I will make during final week for our class.

I rated it a 6 for difficulty,
5 for description
6 for price
7 for the time to prepare

The scale I used was 1-10, a 10 being very good. My overall opinion about this particular recipe was good.

DEEP DISH APPLE PIE

"But Aunt Jenny, I'm scared stiff of pastry making! And Jack's boss is coming to dinner. Gee, I wish I could make pie like you do."

"Helen, I'll show you how easy a pie can be with my can't fail method. Just follow my pointers, and you'll get topnotch pastry every time."

That afternoon: "Each step's so easy! From now on I'll give my husband home-made pies often."

Later that night: "What a swell pie, hon. And did you see how the boss praised your cooking!"

Another meal, another job, another marriage saved by Aunt Jenny. This lovely lady was the young homemaker's fictional friend from Lever Brothers. her job in life was to enlighten the innocent about Spry shortening. Unlike Betty Crocker, who at the time was quite svelte, Jenny was a cushiony old thing, like Uncle Ben if he had been white and female.

Aunt Jenny's 1949 book, *Enjoy Good Eating Every Day*, intersperses recipes for pies and cakes with turgid household melodramas in which nervous wives learn the secrets of winning compliments from husbands, in-laws, bosses, and even children. ("Shortcake for me, mom!" . . . "Man, you should taste my wife's French fries!" . . . "Why, Helen, Jack didn't tell us you were such an expert cook.")

From the gleaming white Spry kitchens ("set off by vibrant color accents of aquamarine and maroon"), where a staff of trained home economists test and retest recipes with scientific precision, comes Aunt Jenny's best recipe for deep dish apple pie. "So digestible you can eat all you want!"

Pie Shell (for a top crust only—this pie is bottomless; for a two-crust pie, double measurements)

1¼ cups sifted all-purpose flour	⅓ cup Spry shortening
½ teaspoon salt	2½ tablespoons ice-cold water

• Mix flour and salt. Cut in two-thirds of the Spry, using a food processor or by hand, until mixture is as fine as meal. Cut in remaining Spry to size of large peas. Do not overmix.

Sprinkle water over mixture. Mix thoroughly with food processor or fork just until all particles cling together in a dough. Take up in hands and shape into smooth ball. Chill 30 minutes.

Remove dough from refrigerator and place on floured board. Roll into rectangle 10 by 8 inches, ⅛ inch thick, or large enough to cover baking dish.

Preheat oven to 425°

Figure 4-21.

My teacher Mrs. Carol Porter read us some background on your life such as your teaching and counseling. I've read two of your books and I notice that when Willie ran away he was using the name Louie Banks. I was wondering if both characters are based on real life experiences and did you know both people before you wrote both books? I was wondering from *Running Loose* was the story about the popcorn and the girl a true story, or was it made up? Also, why did you choose for Louie not to lose his virginity when he was with Becky at the cabin? I read this in my reading class and all the "guys" were upset at the fact that he didn't take advantage of the opportunity that he had. I, myself, thought that it took a lot of character for him to make that choice. Was his choice made based on the actual person or your choice?

In *Running Loose* why didn't Louie speak out when coach Lednecky was telling them to take out Washington? I mean the whole time Louie knew it was wrong but I think he was afraid to tell the truth, or he still could have told Norm. I don't see how Jasper could just sit there when you could tell that he knew that Louie was telling the truth. That and I was just waiting for Carter or Coach Madison to speak out on Louie's behalf? I was also wondering if

Figure 4-22.

you were Coach Madison? If so, why did Louie wait so long to talk to him. I don't think it was fair the way Louie had to train alone, I mean he as still part of the team. But then again, I think it was better for him because he could psych himself up.

Since I'm going to be in Mrs. Porter's class again next year, could you please send your response to the school? I would like to share your answers with my class in September.

Sincerely,

Lisa Salazar

P.S.
Mrs. Porter wants to know if you will be speaking in the Chicago area next year. We would like to plan for a field trip or maybe we could invite you to our school.

Chris Crutcher's response is shown in Figure 4-25. (Chris Crutcher visited our high school in April 1993 as the result of a generous monetary gift from a school board member. Although Lisa had graduated two years earlier, she returned to attend his session, meet him personally, and have him autograph her favorite novels.)

Figure 4-23.

Quotations

Students might have been affected by a specific portion of their reading or from something they heard someone say. These quotes can be displayed in the portfolio. This is true of Eryn as she read *Message from Nam* by Danielle Steele. She felt she gained an understanding of Vietnam through her inter-action with the characters, especially by reflecting on the quotes that she found most memorable at the end of each reading session (see Figure 4-26).

SELECTING MEANINGFUL ARTIFACTS

We use our photo album example with the students to get them to think of their folders as their picture drawers. Just as they would select the most memorable pictures to place in their albums, we ask them to choose artifacts from their folders to put into their portfolios. As they begin making their choices, we share why some of the documents in their folders are more meaningful than others and they generate a list of these reasons to display in the classroom, which we update as new reasons emerge. Although no two classes have the same explanations for the choices they make, the following responses are a sampling from one portfolio session:

- The idea, topic, or theme was one that I liked.
- The paper or project was one that I experimented with in some way.
- The artifact represents a memorable experience (a person, place, or event) and when I look at it or re-read it, memories come back that I enjoy reliving.
- The artifact represents a gratifying learning experience.
- As a result of the paper, reading, project, or inquiry, I changed in some way—it had a lasting effect on me.
- The changes between the first and final draft of a written piece are extensive because of the revisions that took place.
- There was a higher level of commitment to the project than was previously given to others.
- The paper expresses my emotions and/or is unique in some way.
- A new approach was used in the writing or reading.
- The artifact displays my strengths and/or development as a learner.

Teachers can only make a shallow guess at the significance particular learning experiences might have had on their students; however, when learners choose, the process of self-evaluation as it connects to their past, present, and future is made possible.

Some of the most thoughtful portfolios are those in which students have developed a strategy for capturing their immediate reaction to an artifact as soon as they choose it. Unfortunately, reflections and choices take place at the same time. Unless we as teachers and students can determine strategies to help learners dig below the surface of their thoughts to discover why the piece of writing, picture, or journal entry stands apart from the rest when the choice is made, the reason is often lost. Choosing is easy; asking why the choice was made might be difficult for some students. Even more difficult is getting students to decide how they are now different as a result of the learning experience. For example, students might immediately chose a specific book as their favorite or as one that had a lasting effect on them; however, deciding why that book was a favorite or determining how their favorite book changed them will be more difficult. Kristi is an example of a student who initially was only able to identify that *At Risk*, by Alice Hoffman, was her favorite book. As she began to put her portfolio together and worked to extend her initial reactions, several reasons for this reaction, shown in Figure 4-27, surfaced: a field trip was involved, she was proud of her journal entries, and the book helped her cope with a tragic loss she had just experienced.

Large sticky tabs, notebooks, or even tape recorders have worked well for getting at why an artifact is memorable and how the learner changed. When students share their insights and analysis with classmates as they sort through their folders, opportunities arise to understand how other language

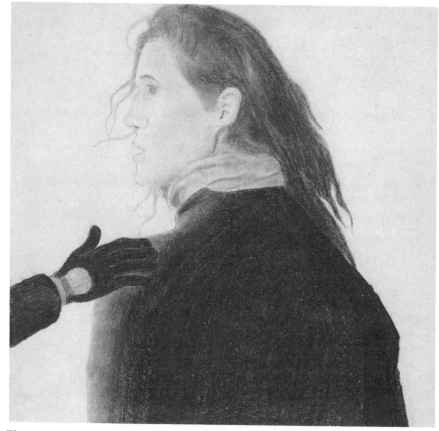

Figure 4-24.

users have developed. They can explore their learning process and the resulting development as they extend their initial reactions.

We are thankful for the freedom we had in our teaching situation and that we did not have to use portfolios for accountability reasons. The chance to discover that students need a voice in the process might not have happened if we had perceived ourselves limited to traditional assessment measures. In our effort to put the learner, and therefore choice, before any other purposes, we found that the portfolio could be used as a learning strategy that supported reflexivity. When other purposes guide the use and/or reason for the portfolio, the possibilities for self-discovery during the learning process are greatly diminished. As teachers, schools, and districts experiment with alternative forms of assessment, they are now asking if it is possible to create a portfolio that serves dual purposes. Can a balance between accountability and student choice exist in harmony? For example, if a teacher

Dear Lisa,

Thanks for your good words about my books. I wasn't the fastest reader in the world when I was in high school, either, so it's nice to know *Running Loose* and *Crazy Horse* worked for you. You may not be fast, but you're observant. Not many people notice that I used Louie's name in *Crazy Horse*. In some ways both characters are based on real life experiences, but not in the sense that everything that happened to them happened to me. Most fiction writers like to use their imaginations by taking small things from real life and creating stories out of them.

The popcorn story in *Running Loose* is not a true story. It is sort of a myth that boys like to tell when they're building themselves up. I heard that story when I was in the fifth grade, and I believed it was true. The problem is, it's a story that is degrading to girls, and I wanted anyone else who heard about or read it, to know that: that it's a story for braggers. I chose for Louie not to lose his virginity at the cabin with Becky because I wanted to talk about how scary sexual stuff can be when you're not ready for it. It could have gone either way and would have been believable, but everybody writes it the other way. I can remember being very confused about sex, and wishing there weren't so much pressure to be some kind of hot shot--so I wrote it that way.

The reason Louie didn't speak out against Lednecky at first was because he was afraid. We are taught not to question adults sometimes, and most of us are afraid to be embarrassed or called "wussy". I figured it would take a guy like Louie some time to work up his courage.

No, I'm not Coach Madison, but he said some things I believe. He's a character I like a lot and there's certainly *some* of me in him. But there's some of me in Dakota, too, and in Louie's father, and unfortunately probably Lednecky and Jasper too. It would be nice if we were all one way or the other, but we're not.

You can tell Mrs. Porter that I will be in Decatur next year on the first of November. I think that's not close to Chicago, but I'll bet I have to go through Chicago to get there. Her best bet is to call Greenwillow Books, or contact me personally at the address on the envelope.

Thanks again for taking time to write. You ask *very* good questions.

Sincerely,

Chris Crutcher

Figure 4-25.

believes that a student has not chosen a piece of writing that displays an achievement worth noting, should the teacher include that piece? If the teacher chooses, should the teacher be responsible for the narrative that is included in the portfolio for this piece? To answer these questions we need to return to the biography and autobiography examples that illustrate the differences between the types of portfolios that can be assembled.

If we were writing our autobiography, we would choose the meaningful episodes of our lives to relate to an audience and each choice would be the

Message From Mom
Memorable Quote

Chapter 24
pg. 330, paragraph 3
"A 'stupid thing' ... a stupid thing ...
wasn't it always a stupid thing?
Was there an intelligent way to die
here? By friendly fire or plastic
bomb in a restaurant or howitzer
or land mine? What was smart
about any of it? What difference
did it make when it was all over?"

I thought this was a particularly
important quote from Paxton because it
sums up how pointless and stupid the
war was! Paxton was an expert on this
because Peter was killed by friendly fire —
he was shot by another American soldier
because he was mistaken for a Viet Cong.
Ralph was killed by a bomb which
just happened to be placed in his
car. France, who was young and
beautiful, killed herself & children
which was very stupid. The last sentence
means at the end of the war all the
deaths added up to nothing. We still
lost the war that went on for years.

Figure 4-26.

The book At Risk was my favorite book all year. I chose this book when we went on our field trip to the book store. I think that in these journal entries I really expressed myself and told how I felt. At first all I was doing was summarizing and giving personal connections but by the end I think that I was Predicting and asking more questions. This book really helped me a lot because of what happened in the book, especially how to deal with death.

Figure 4-27.

starting point for personal analysis. Conversely, when someone else attempts to create meaning for and about us through a biography, they have their own ideas about the importance of various episodes in our lives. This may make for interesting reading or it may meet district guidelines, but rarely would personal value surface in terms of learning. When choice is taken out of the students' hands, we believe that the purposes for such an action need to be established with all those involved in the learning. Further, educators need to acknowledge that when student choice and, therefore, voice is removed, the portfolio as a learning strategy no longer exists. Under these circumstances the portfolio reverts to a storage/accountability folder whose value for learning is lost.

As we search for those ways to value learning, the following questions arise:

- What are some strategies for helping students capture their thoughts and analyze the reasons behind their choices?
- How can we analyze the choices our students have made in terms of moving curriculum forward?
- What instructional implications do our students' choices of artifacts reveal?
- Will alternative modes for presenting portfolios alter the types of artifacts that students will be able to choose?

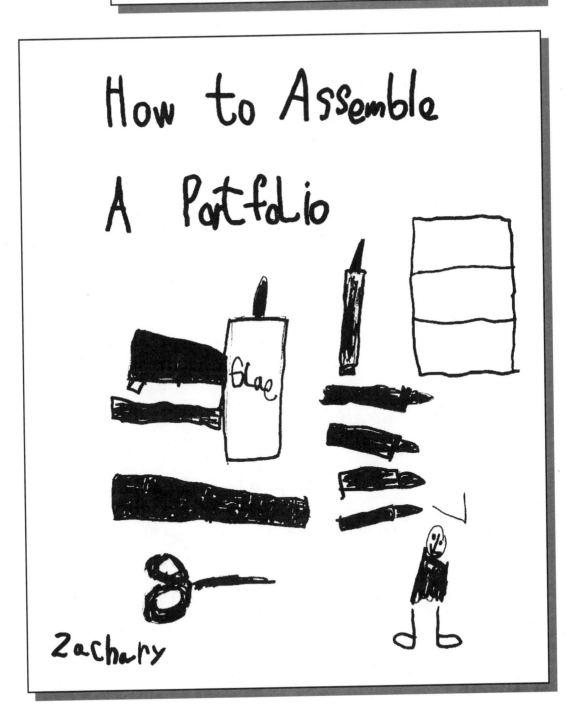

RECALL THE DAY when you decide it is finally time to organize the famous "picture drawer." You choose a spot on the floor, dump the contents, and begin reliving events and recalling people. Chances are you want to draw others into your experiences and tell them what you remember about your favorite pictures. You are probably less likely to search for paper and pen to quietly record your feelings.

Students will react in much the same way as they open their folders (the class counterpart to the picture drawer) where they have collected artifacts over a period of time. Authors' circle comments, written conversations, and reflections on discussion reveal the impact students have on each other's learning. The room will be filled with oral reflections: "Listen to this" and "I don't believe I said this" and an occasional "I forgot how good this was." The students will not likely grab a sheet of paper to record their initial reactions. Since, however, we value the role social interaction plays in the learning process, we have found that the most important component we can provide during those first days of folder exploration is plenty of time and space to relive and recall the people and events that are associated with the artifacts students discover in their folders.

Another by-product of this public-sharing process is that students may gain insight into themselves and their learning that they would not have explored in the isolation of their home. As students spread their work out around them, it becomes routine to share with a neighbor what they chose to include in their portfolio and why they chose it. Each student benefits in the process: one is allowed to give an oral first draft of the reflection he may include with the artifact, and from this reflection the other student may gain an idea for something to look for within her own work. Often this sharing is extended into an informal authors' circle as one student questions another about their explanation or even offers suggestions about why a piece should be included in the portfolio. Ideas that may not even be fully formed when the students begin their explanation are shaped and revised as those ideas are shared with other learners. The sense of community present in the classroom during the entire process makes any confusion and noise worthwhile. After trying several strategies to record the reactions of students as they begin to sort through, share, and organize the contents of their folders, we have decided that video taping may be the most effective way to capture those valuable initial responses.

One of the areas where our present view of portfolios differs most markedly from our initial view is the identification of the portfolio audience. When our view of audience changed, so did our purpose for compiling the portfolio. Our students had been writing for authentic audiences and for real purposes all semester, but we reverted to our traditional method of having students turn in their portfolios for us to grade at the end of their scheduled exam time. Although the *form* of the exam had changed dramatically, the traditional *purpose* with a teacher-audience remained intact. We sent our students a mixed message, and the problems this created were most easily observed through the reflections they included with each entry in their portfolio.

All the wonderful oral reflections we had overheard during the selection process were nowhere to be found in those entries. Those insights seemed lost forever because the students obviously felt they need not record them for us since we had celebrated the changes and development with them throughout the semester and while they reflected orally on their choices. They knew we would understand what they were trying to say and that we could fill in the gray areas with our own memories because we had been there with them. This situation is reminiscent of our "picture drawer" and all the photos we never took time to write on when they first returned from being developed—the time when our reflections would have been most meaningful and most detailed. We assumed that we would always remember why we originally snapped that picture and that other viewers of our photo album would be able to appreciate our choices.

The students' reflections were filled with the same assumptions, and in the present form, these reflections would mean very little by the time our students returned to them the following semester or the next school year. How could we encourage students to extend their reflections so they could return to them at a later time and benefit from complete and thoughtful responses?

The answer seemed to lie in the portfolio audience. When the students realized that we were the only ones who would ever read or share what they had discovered about their learning, their commitment to the reflection process was minimal. With our next round of portfolios, we explored ways to introduce the portfolio to an authentic audience, just as we had done with all our work throughout the semester. We began to discuss the portfolio as the autobiography of one's learning, suggesting that anyone who picked up the portfolio should be able to follow the story of the student's learning for that semester. Students began to see the importance of clearly articulating their story in order for the reader to see them as the learner they were, the learner they had become, and the learner they are striving to be. By making the reflections public, we found students working to justify the choices they made, and as a result of this detailed articulation they gained a greater understanding of their own learning process. By redefining and extending the audience, the portfolios evolved into a tool for thinking; students explored and discovered facets of their learning that previously had gone unrecorded.

With these revisions in audience and purpose, we turned to the actual logistics of assembling the portfolio. Of course, the first attempt was our most difficult because it brought with it unexplored territory. How should a portfolio look? What format should it follow? Someone had to be "first" to

Figure 5-1.

create the models that would be copied, modified, or rejected by students to come. However, two questions eventually evolved that provided us and our students with guidance concerning format: If the portfolios were piled on a table, which one would you be most likely to pick up? Once you started reading that portfolio, what would make you want to continue? These questions led the students to discover the importance of an attractive cover.

Many of our students pointed out that, initially, they reached for a novel because of the way it looked; therefore, they needed to consider the same principle when designing their portfolio cover. At this point we began to hone our skills as scavengers. Any scrap of paper or yarn could be just what was needed to add the finishing touch to a portfolio. We piled a table with all the material we could gather: construction paper, tape, glue, colored pencils, crayons, markers, typing paper of several colors, yarn, ribbon, clear divider pages, stencils, etc. Some students chose to decorate the cover of a three-ring binder; others created covers from construction paper and bound them with yarn or ribbon or metal rings. Many of our students preferred using our newly purchased binding machine. The plastic spirals seem to lend an air of professionalism to the entire process. And, of course, there are those who hurriedly scribbled "My Portfolio" on the outside of a file folder and crammed everything inside. See Figure 5-1 for samples of portfolio covers.

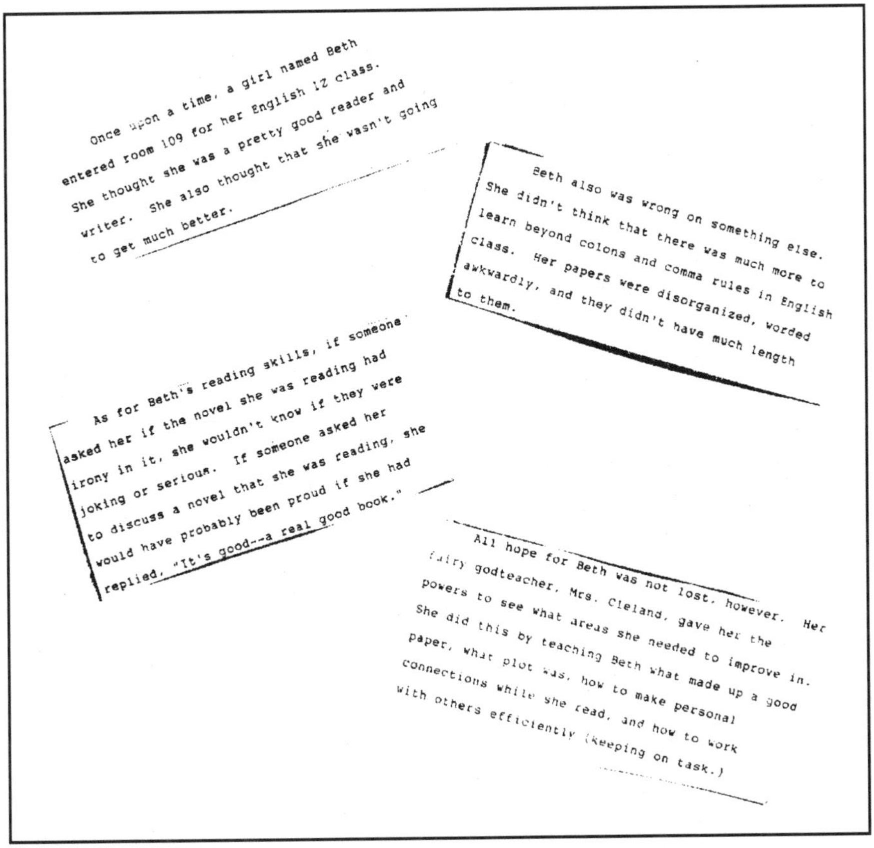

Once upon a time, a girl named Beth entered room 109 for her English 12 class. She thought she was a pretty good reader and writer. She also thought that she wasn't going to get much better.

Beth also was wrong on something else. She didn't think that there was much more to learn beyond colons and comma rules in English class. Her papers were disorganized, worded awkwardly, and they didn't have much length to them.

As for Beth's reading skills, if someone asked her if the novel she was reading had irony in it, she wouldn't know if they were joking or serious. If someone asked her to discuss a novel that she was reading, she would have probably been proud if she had replied, "It's good—a real good book."

All hope for Beth was not lost, however. Her fairy godteacher, Mrs. Cleland, gave her the powers to see what areas she needed to improve in. She did this by teaching Beth what made up a good paper, what plot was, how to make personal connections while she read, and how to work with others efficiently (keeping on task.)

Figure 5-2.

Once the reader has chosen your portfolio, how can you sustain interest in your learning story? The answer to this question seemed to lie in the word, *story*. If you think of the portfolio as a way of sharing the story of your learning with anyone who picks it up, then you must first invite the readers into your story—make them want to read on (exactly what we had discovered during the semester about any effective introduction). As students began to experiment with an opening page we referred to as the "Invitation to the Reader," the format of the portfolios began to change dramatically. With each new round of portfolios, students became more and more creative about the ways they invited their readers into their portfolios. Many times that first invitation set the stage for the theme of a student's entire portfolio.

Beth chose to present her portfolio, seen in Figure 5-2, in third person in the form of a fairy tale. In Figure 5-3, Gwen invites her readers to access her portfolio file. Lynne was the first student to present her portfolio as a script

```
Computer Data Base ELS:

File Access Code #1267517.

Accessing:

File #1267517.

Name: Gwendolyn
Sex: Female
Race: Caucasian
Age: 17
Weight: 140
Height: 64 inches
Birthdate:
Current Residence:




Current Grade Status: 11th grade
Currently Enrolled at Mundelein High School, Mundelein, Il.




Previous writing experience:
        Started writing poetry at the age of 12. Won honorable
mention in a writing contest for a poem titled,
"If I were a color." Unusual sucess with grade-school level
English courses. Graduated salutatorian of 26 in graduating
class and went on to honors English at        South High School
taught under        Recieved an A and a B. Transferred to
Mundelein High School sophomore year and entered honors
English under        Subject apparently likes to write and
to read. Is currently enrolled under Mrs. Porter for senior
Composition.
```

Figure 5-3.

to a play, shown in Figure 5-4, and many students have followed her example in the past three years. Lisa's portfolio was entitled "The Footsteps of My Growth," and her invitation to the reader was written on a footstep reinforcing her theme (see Figure 5-5).

Knowing that readers would need guidance as they progressed through the story, students began to add divider pages to precede the artifact the reader was about to experience. The divider pages usually gave the reader the background information necessary to understand what they were about

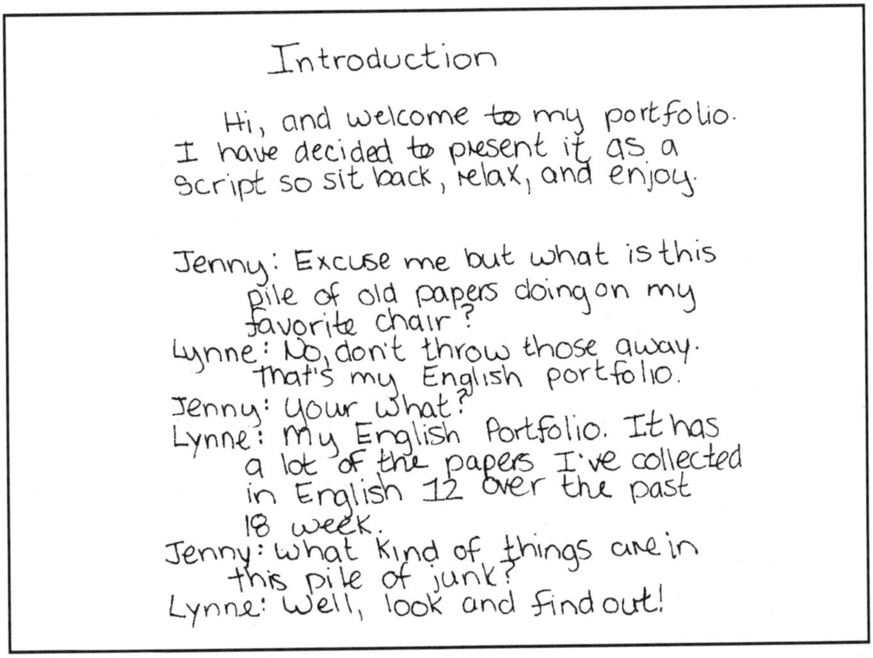

Introduction

Hi, and welcome to my portfolio. I have decided to present it as a script so sit back, relax, and enjoy.

Jenny: Excuse me but what is this pile of old papers doing on my favorite chair?

Lynne: No, don't throw those away. That's my English portfolio.

Jenny: Your what?

Lynne: My English Portfolio. It has a lot of the papers I've collected in English 12 over the past 18 week.

Jenny: What kind of things are in this pile of junk?

Lynne: Well, look and find out!

Figure 5-4.

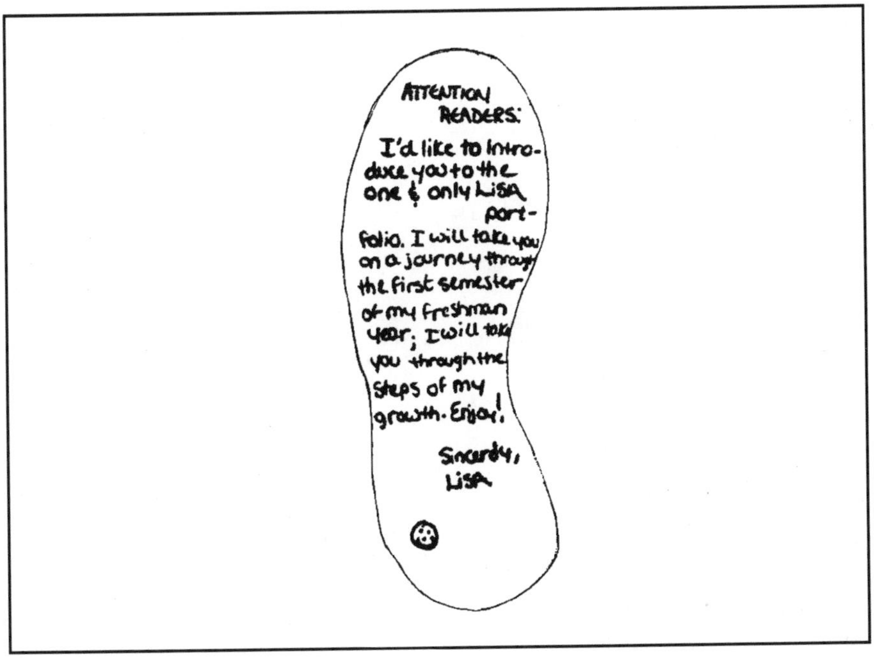

Figure 5-5.

Access writing history for code #1267517 under Porter file.

Accessing:

file #1 of #1267517

Type: Free Write

Subject: Short Story titled "Mine on Thursdays"

Run Analysis on file #1

Strong introduction. Background of main characters is strong, however, story fails to flow smoothly. Jerky and sudden paragraph change lacks the transition that is needed to familiarize the reader with the story. The conclusion is sudden, not long enough and does not conclude the paper with the proper smoothness.

Figure 5-6.

Interview

Jenny: Well, what is this?
Lynne: This is my first piece of writing. When we first entered the class, we were immediately matched with someone we didn't know. Our first assignment was to write about that person.
Jenny: (sarcastic) o-neat-o! Was it fun?
Lynne: Well, I liked being paired up with someone I didn't know and then getting to know them but I didn't end up getting too much detail about my partner.
Jenny: Well, make up your mind, did you like it or not?
Lynne: It was fun but looking back on it now. I wrote a very elementary piece. There wasn't anything really interesting about this piece to make the reader want to keep going.
Jenny: All right, before you give it all away, let me read it.

Figure 5-7.

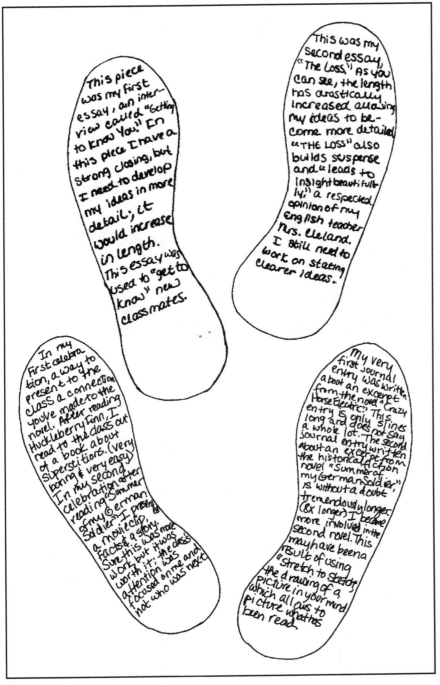

This piece was my first essay, an interview called "Getting to know you!" In this piece I have a strong closing, but I need to develop my ideas in more detail; it would increase in length. This essay was used to "get to know" new classmates.

This was my second essay, "The Loss." As you can see, the length has drastically increased allowing my ideas to become more detailed. "THE LOSS" also builds suspense and "leads to insight beautifully," a respected opinion of my English teacher Mrs. Eveland. I still need to work on stating clearer ideas.

In my first celebration, a way to present to the class a connection you've made to the novel. After reading Huckleberry Finn, I read to the class out of a book about superstitions. (very boring & very easy) In my second celebration after reading Summer of my German Soldier, I presented a movie clip, facts & a story. Sure this was more work, but it; the class attention was focused on me and not who was next.

My very first journal entry was written about an excerpt from the novel "Crazy Horse Electric." This entry is only 5 lines long and does not say a whole lot. The second journal entry written about an excerpt from the historical fiction novel "Summer of my German Soldier," is without a doubt tremendously longer. (8x longer) I became more involved in the second novel. This may have been a result of using "stretch to sketch," the drawing of a picture in your mind which allows to picture what has been read.

Figure 5-8.

Figure 5-9.

to read. Students might explain the strategy, the assignment, when it was completed, who worked with them—whatever information they deemed necessary to effectively introduce each artifact. After this divider page is read and turned, readers find the artifact in its entirety (sample artifacts listed in Chapter 4). The response following the artifact is one component from our first attempt at portfolios that remained unchanged. In their response, students explain why they chose the piece, and what they discovered about themselves by reflecting on the experience associated with that piece.

In Figure 5-6, Gwen continues her computer file format to introduce her first artifact. Figure 5-7 shows how Lynne continues her script with the scene that introduces her first piece of writing: the interview and, in Figure 5-8, Lisa's footsteps continue to guide the reader through her portfolio. Ingrid entitled her portfolio "Around the World," and each divider page, shown in Figure 5-9, stopped at a new destination that related somehow to the artifact she was introducing.

At some point in the process of compiling the portfolio, it is important for the teacher and student to return to our working definition of a portfolio: a collection of artifacts accompanied by a reflective narrative that not only helps the learner to understand and extend learning, but also invites the

After reading the last journal entry, I hope you appreciated the letter you just read that I wrote later in the semester. I wrote a letter! The things that is surprising is that it was about a book that I disliked the ending of. I actually surprised myself by doing this. I am also proud of myself because two years ago this day I could not read a book at all. Now I am reading 2 books every six weeks. Pretty good for a person who couldn't read for 5 minutes. The journal entry you just read was a piece of garbage. It was another case of me having no idea about the story because I did not care. I could not say anything because I did not know what it was about. I am just glad that my journal entries have gotten better and completer. This is embarrassing to show.

Figure 5-10.

> I feel that this paper was good for a first paper of the year but could use a lot of work. I need to work on using my commas into the sentences much better. That is the my biggest problem in all my papers. I think that my theme of using the diary worked out well in the end. It made the paper much easier to write. I thought that the interviewing part of the project was fun to do because the atmosphere was real easy going. We were allowed to work at our own pace which really helped a lot. In the future another thing I need to work on is the answering of "why" of all my statements
>
> *Final Reflection.*

Figure 5-11.

reader of the portfolio to gain insights about learning and the learner. The danger of stopping at the phrase, "a collection of artifacts," seems ever present. Students can become so involved in creating and decorating cover and divider pages that the real essence of the portfolio may become secondary: the reflective narrative. As our colleague bemoaned in Chapter 3, they may look beautiful but say absolutely nothing.

Our students frequently needed to be reminded that *each* artifact they chose to include in their portfolio should be accompanied by a narrative explaining why they chose it and what it illustrates about their learning. The narrative's form was usually determined by the format or theme the student had chosen for the entire portfolio. We discovered that it was often necessary to discuss the qualities of an effective reflection or to examine sample reflections on the overhead projector to determine which ones better inform not only the learner but the reader of the portfolio.

Mike included the reflection, shown in Figure 5-10, to follow his journal entries as a way to draw conclusions about how he had changed as a reader.

After introducing each piece, Lisa included the artifact in a pocket across from the introduction. On the pocket, Lisa wrote a final reflection (see Figure 5-11) about each artifact that included what she realized about her own learning as a result of examining that artifact.

Thank you for taking the time to look through my portfolio! Hopefully you thought i made as much progress as i thought i did. Not only have my writing skills improved immensely, but i have learned how to read and understand books better. i have also learned how to speak effectively in front of people. i am really impressed with how easily i was able to see all the improvement that i have made. Did you see all the places where i need to make more progress? One place i need to work on is personal connections. In the future, i would like to work on making more personal connections when i am reading books. i feel that this is a very important step in drawing yourself into the book. i also hope that i get more chances to speak in front of my classmates so that if i actually have to speak in public, i don't get quite so nervous. i would also like to make another portfolio in the future because i think that it really helps students see how much progress they have made.

Figure 5-12.

Students close their portfolio with a reflection that summarizes their discoveries about themselves and about their learning. They comment on the changes they have seen in reading, writing, speaking, and listening, and they set goals for themselves in each of those areas. This chapter of their autobiography is completed, and with the shift in purpose and audience the end product becomes something the students can return to throughout the next semester or the coming year. The reflections will provide them with a

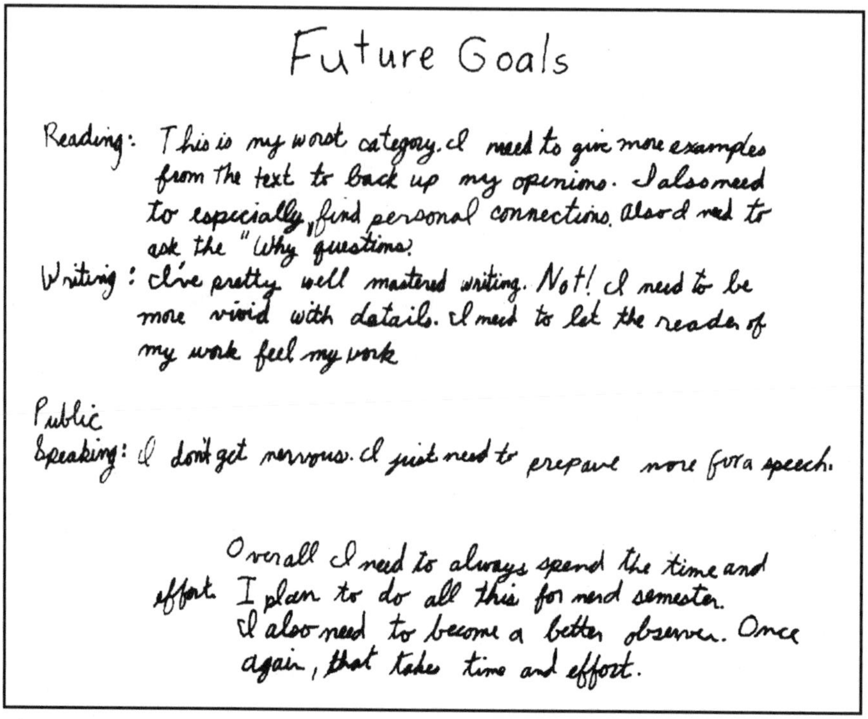

Future Goals

Reading: This is my worst category. I need to give more examples from the text to back up my opinions. I also need to especially find personal connections. I also need to ask the "why questions."

Writing: I've pretty well mastered writing. Not! I need to be more vivid with details. I need to let the reader of my work feel my work.

Public
Speaking: I don't get nervous. I just need to prepare more for a speech.

Overall I need to always spend the time and effort. I plan to do all this for next semester. I also need to become a better observer. Once again, that takes time and effort.

Figure 5-13.

complete picture of where they were as learners during that time in their educational career.

It's the addition of the reflections that sets the portfolio apart from the picture album. The album allows the audience to make observations about a person's life by drawing their own conclusions as they progress through the photographs. The portfolio incorporates the authors' voice to guide the reader through their learning, while allowing the author to make their own discoveries about their learning process.

Britt's and Dave's closing reflections, illustrated in Figures 5-12 and 5-13, reveal not only their goals but also allow the reader to see their personality. Britt is outgoing and loves to talk, and her conversational reflection highlights that love. Dave is a talented science student and his straightforward, analytical style reflects his love in that area.

Maybe the most effective way to illustrate the difference between an album/scrapbook and a portfolio is to share the reflective components of one student's portfolio. Hemal chose a concise format that illustrates his complete understanding of his learning process. In Figure 5-14 he introduces each artifact, shows that artifact, and then reflects on what that artifact reveals about his learning.

My Portfolio

by:
Hemal

Dear Reader,
    This is a portfolio that highlights all my growth during the past eighteen weeks. This folder is a guide for you to check up on my progress and see how I reacted to the many different things that we did. Also, you will get a grasp on some of the tactics used in the discussion process and the writing. It is a guide which shows some of my papers, tells how I felt about each piece, and how I improved on every piece. It also tells how I changed as a reader, and all my improvements from one book to the next. There are many things that I have learned, but I know that there are still many more things that I have to work on. So sit back and enjoy.

                                        Hemal

    This was the first paper that I did at the beginning of the year. It is an interview on one of my classmates and was used as a acquaintance piece which brought us closer together...

    . . . I chose this piece so that you could get a grip on where I was at the beginning of the year. I feel that I wasn't in top form when I wrote this essay. As I look through it now, I see that I didn't have as many drafts as I did in my later essays. This essay wasn't as descriptive and detailed as I had hoped. This paper was written from notes and I really didn't like the form. I thought that my later essays turned out better because they had been through many more drafts and through author's circles which helped us guide our ideas. It also let us understand how other classmates reacted to our work.

Figure 5-14.

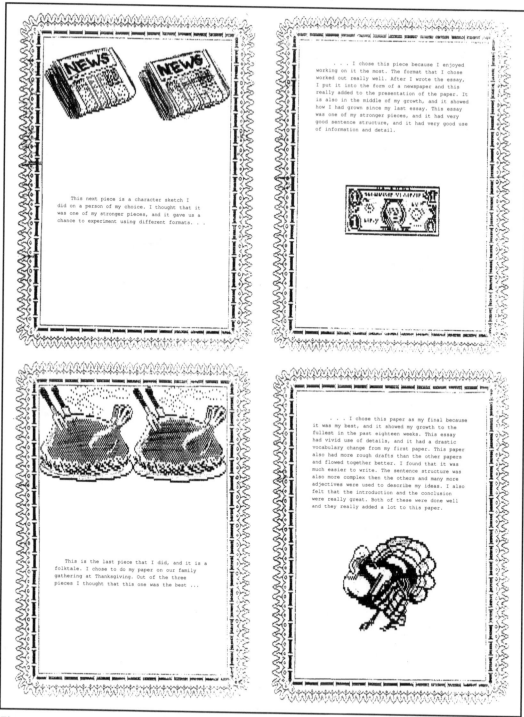

This next piece is a character sketch I did on a person of my choice. I thought that it was one of my stronger pieces, and it gave us a chance to experiment using different formats. . .

. . . I chose this piece because I enjoyed working on it the most. The format that I chose worked out really well. After I wrote the essay, I put it into the form of a newspaper and this really added to the presentation of the paper. It is also in the middle of my growth, and it showed how I had grown since my last essay. This essay was one of my stronger pieces, and it had very good sentence structure, and it had very good use of information and detail.

This is the last piece that I did, and it is a folktale. I chose to do my paper on our family gathering at Thanksgiving. Out of the three pieces I thought that this one was the best ...

. . . I chose this paper as my final because it was my best, and it showed my growth to the fullest in the past eighteen weeks. This essay had vivid use of details, and it had a drastic vocabulary change from my first paper. This paper also had more rough drafts than the other papers and flowed together better. I found that it was much easier to write. The sentence structure was also more complex then the others and many more adjectives were used to describe my ideas. I also felt that the introduction and the conclusion were really great. Both of these were done well and they really added a lot to this paper.

Figure 5-14 cont'd.

This next section is an example of the kinds of journal entries that we did in the past eighteen weeks. The first one is on one of the earlier books that I read, and the second is on the last book that I read...

. . . I chose these journal entries so that I can tell how I have improved as a reader. The first ones show that when I read I used to summarize what I read, and the later ones show that as I read, I looked deeper and tried to make personal connections. I tried to react to the characters, and I really got into the book. I also tried to make predictions on what would happen as the book progressed and what would happen to the characters as they went on. Also, my discussions were more interesting as I started to read more closely. We used different styles of discussion, and I found it worked out really well. I really enjoy reading, and I also read more closely.

This was a portfolio that told about my progressions during the past eighteen weeks. I have grown in many areas, and I find myself still changing in many ways. I see that my papers are getting better because I am trying to use more details, have a more complex sentence structure, use strong adjectives, and I have a vocabulary change. Also, when I read I find that I try to pay attention to details and try to draw a picture in my mind as I read. I try to make connections to the characters and try to make predictions. In the past eighteen weeks, I have grown many ways but this is just the beginning, and I know that I still have a long way to go and many more things to improve on.

Figure 5-14 cont'd.

OUR DESKS WERE piled to a teetering height with our students' first portfolios; most teachers had long since left for home after a day of administering and grading objective exams. There we were, reading and sharing the responses in our students' portfolios when Carol came to the last page of Deeana's, shown in Figure 6-1. Carol's first thought was, "Yes Deeana, you do ask good questions!" She read the entry to Janell.

As a result of Deeana's question, we immediately began to search under the clutter for a clean sheet of paper to begin planning the revisions for our next portfolio attempt. We may have met the requirements of our school district by using the portfolio as an alternative assessment instrument, but we hadn't considered other possibilities for the students until we read that simple question tucked at the end of Deeana's portfolio. We decided to respond to each student's portfolio.

Today, we write to our students either on one of the sign-in sheets they provide at the end of the portfolio or on our own sheet of paper, which we tuck between their pages. We respond to the students' reflections on their learning in the same way that someone would respond to a letter received from a friend.

Prior to displaying one of his pieces of writing, Rob invited the reader of his portfolio to provide feedback (see Figure 6-2). On the blank sheet that Rob had promised to put at the end of his portfolio, a reminder was written to the reader (see Figure 6-3).

> This semester I discovered that I am not a mystery writter! I lack the cleverness and expertise it takes to create such writing. I am blind or naive or oblivious to the clues given in mysteries but I never see the murderer or any evidence until after the information is given. It's quite agrivating because I really enjoy reading mysteries. I like writing about real life situations. although I do like to add some imagination. Just enough so that the story is still realistic. My writing changed gramatically quite a bit as well as in completness, and discription. I don't think my journal writing changed much though. I think I basically always had good ideas and questions. What do you think?

Figure 6-1.

The next story I wrote is the longest I have ever written. Except for the book I am putting out about my feelings life which will be aviclable by Sept.

This story took alot out of my ideas and put them into one I took from things that have happened to me, places I have been, and books I have read. It was by far the easiest to write. The ideas just poured from my head onto the paper.

Now I will stop talking and let you read the piece of writing. Please leave a comment on either piece of paper on the blank sheet directly following this piece

Figure 6-2.

This concludes my writing life, well for 2nd semester anyway. If you have any ideas on how I can improve my writing please call me at   or just write something on the bottom here OK. See you later.

Figure 6-3.

Carol responded,

Rob,

Your SIDS piece was almost a speech in class when you shared it. The information related to the book and helped answer many questions for your classmates. I think you found out how important commitment is to writing this semester. Maybe next year we should work on strategies that will help you get started.

                                                                    cp

When Carol finished reading Angel's portfolio (see his introductory page in Chapter 3, page 46) she wrote:

Angel,

You should be pleased with your progress in writing, speaking, and reading another language. Many students would be afraid to take the chances you are —but you're right about what you said—you learn from your mistakes and the opinions of others. You have taught your classmates a lot about your culture and its values by sharing your life experiences in writing. Thank you for helping them learn, too.

                                                                    cp

Another idea we had at that time was to require the students to share their portfolios with one of their parents and ask the parent to respond to two open-ended questions. At that time it was our belief that questions would provide the parents some guidance in responding, since few had probably seen a learning portfolio, much less been asked to write to the author of one. Jason's mother's response is shown in Figure 6-4.

This time it was Kelly who kept us from getting too smug with our revisions when he asked for a second sheet of questions because he wanted his girlfriend to respond to his portfolio (see Figure 6-5). Obviously, Chris shared, supported, and celebrated Kelly's learning and development. Kelly and Chris also forced us to reevaluate our previous stance, that only teachers and parents respond to the portfolios. Once again, we found that we had set up a learning situation that was not supported by the theoretical beliefs we held and implemented daily in the classroom. By this time in the school year, the students had been creating their personal interpretations of various learning events with the help of their learning community. For example, students had shared their bookmarks with classmates to determine their most common types of responses to literature and then set goals for future responses. We had also encouraged students to extend their sharing to their community beyond the classroom, but when it was time for us to look back at their learning, we excluded these support systems.

Prior to our third portfolio attempt, we asked the students to list those who supported their learning outside the classroom, and who might be interested in reading about their growth, struggles, accomplishments, and

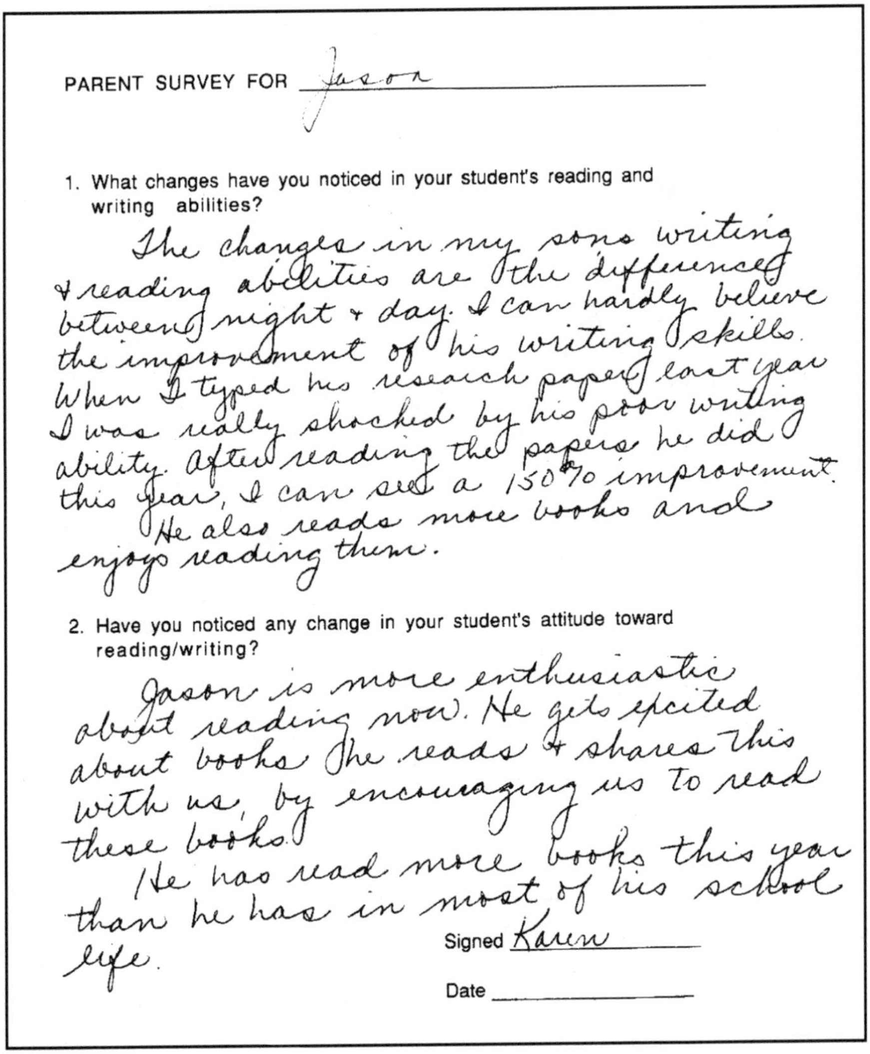

PARENT SURVEY FOR _Jason_

1. What changes have you noticed in your student's reading and writing abilities?

The changes in my sons writing & reading abilities are the difference between night & day. I can hardly believe the improvement of his writing skills. When I typed his research paper last year I was really shocked by his poor writing ability. After reading the papers he did this year, I can see a 150% improvement. He also reads more books and enjoys reading them.

2. Have you noticed any change in your student's attitude toward reading/writing?

Jason is more enthusiastic about reading now. He gets excited about books he reads & shares this with us, by encouraging us to read these books. He has read more books this year than he has in most of his school life.

Signed _Karen_

Date _____

Figure 6-4.

discoveries. Together, we generated a list of the people outside our immediate learning community who helped us accomplish our goals. We (students and teachers) have chosen to share our portfolios with those individuals because they have supported us as learners or have the potential to support us in the future. Our initial fear that people outside our classroom might not know how to respond to a portfolio is now gone. If the student thinks it might be a problem, we as teachers write our note first, to give the reader an idea of what might be an "appropriate" response.

PARENT SURVEY FOR _Kelly_

1. **What changes have you noticed in your student's reading and writing abilities?** There were many changes in Kelly's work. He writes much more fluily and more imaginative. He shows more intellect in his writing and his journals then earlier. It seems that he uses much more detail and it makes if the reader interested to read further. The only thing is his handwriting leaves alot to be desired.

2. **Have you noticed any change in your student's attitude toward reading/writing?** Kelly seems much more interested in reading/writing then before. It's almost a love for reading. It gives him the opportunity to let his imagination take over and he has a wild imagination. I find myself laughing when he reads me one of his stories because he puts so much feeling into it. It makes me happy to see him try so hard.

Signed _____

Date _____

Figure 6-5.

PEOPLE WHO SUPPORT OUR LEARNING

The Teacher

Our students have decided and helped us to understand that teachers should always respond to the portfolio. As much as the student is responsible for learning, the teacher is responsible for supporting and facilitating that learning. This partnership requires constant verbal and written exchanges and the portfolio is a mode for written communication. When students answer the question, "Why did I change? " the teacher gains valuable information concerning the community, risk taking, strategies, skills lessons, materials, and literature that are a part of the curriculum. This information is crucial for teachers when they begin their self-evaluation in their teaching portfolio. Discovering, affirming, and/or negating what worked for the class in general or a student, personally, is both rewarding and disheartening. But it is that important step of departure that is needed to decide what needs to be done next, both for the class and for individual learners. It is in this way that the student's self-evaluation informs curriculum and instruction.

Whenever students listed a piece of literature or a strategy as having an impact on their learning, Janell tallied these to determine if there was a pattern. By drawing conclusions from this tally sheet, Janell gained important information concerning the curriculum and her instruction. She was able to keep some pieces of literature in place and abandon others after analyzing how instruction might have influenced these student choices. She also found that those strategies students hadn't listed were ones that she hadn't reinforced as effectively as she perceived. This tally sheet (shown in Figure 6-6) initiated Janell's reflections that helped her to set instructional goals that she discussed in her portfolio.

The few students who listed reflection as a strategy that had an impact on their learning surprised Janell, and she explored this concern in the following entry in her teaching portfolio:

> My lack of personal reflection is a source of embarrassment. I found some interesting numbers that reveal the impact of my lack of demonstration. When I actively demonstrated poetry writing, 58 of 64 students attempted poetry writing. At the end of the year when I asked students to share which strategies were most effective for them, 3 of 64 mentioned reflections. At the time, I justified these numbers by saying that reflections just hadn't come to mind. Now I think I know why it didn't come to mind. How often did they see me reflecting?

At the end of second semester, Janell wanted to explore a way to coordinate the goals from freshmen year to the beginning of sophomore year. She devised a conference form that the student and she could fill out as they discussed the portfolio. This form, shown in Figure 6-7, could be handed to sophomore teachers to preview over the summer to help them decide what needs to be done with the class and with the individual. A similar form could be adapted for use with a portfolio at any point in the school year.

The Classroom Community

Portfolio Share Day is a time to celebrate learning and a time to learn about and from others. Large tables are set up and, when the students enter the classroom, they find their portfolios on display. Several days are spent reading and responding to the portfolios of the classmates in their community

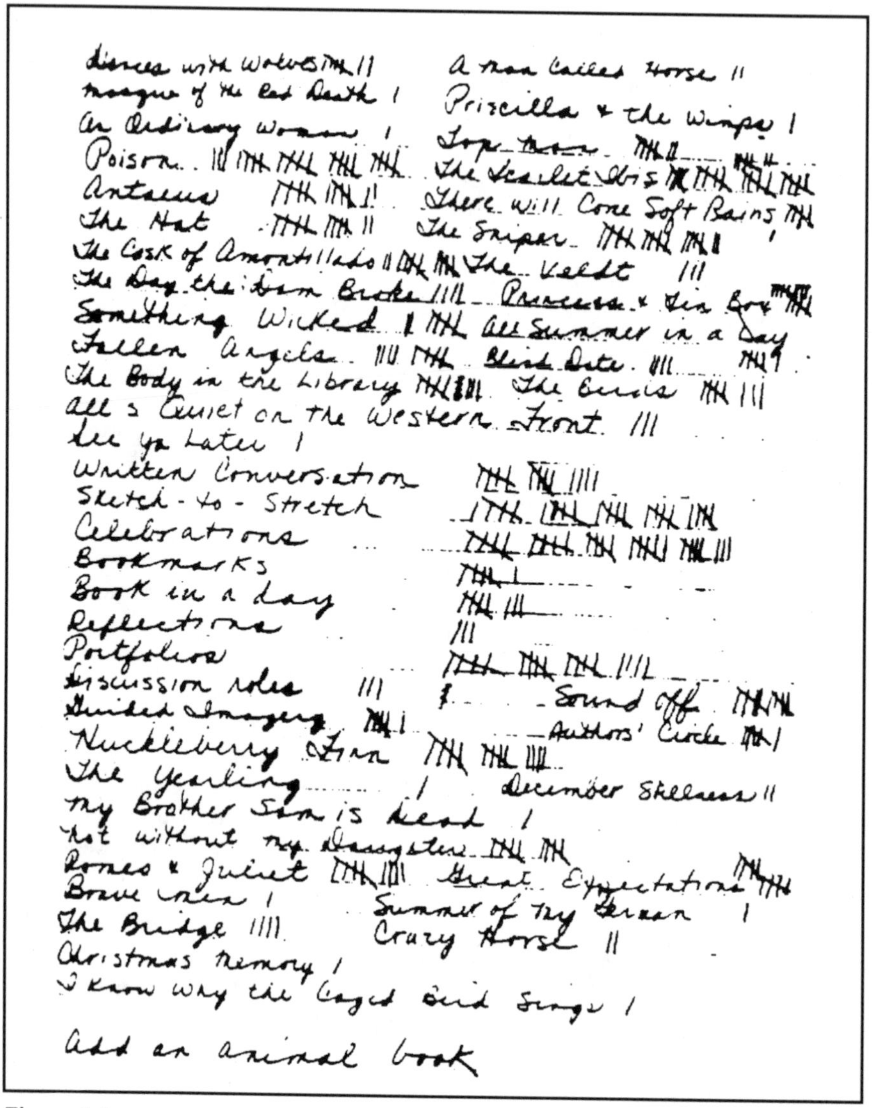

Figure 6-6.

and the authors of a larger community. In our teaching situation, as many as eight classes might use the same room throughout the school day. On one share day, we might put the portfolios from the third period class out for third period only and on another share day all eight sets would be displayed for all eight periods. When students from the same class period share, the readers of the portfolios are able to respond as members of the community who have

Second Semester portfolio observations

What do ___Britt's___ reflections reveal about

his/her learning process:
- she values input from classmates as a part of her revision process
- closing reflections have become an integral part of her learning process. She sets personal goals in all areas as a result of her reflection.

taking responsibility for learning:
- Britt calls her own author's circle out of class as a way of further revising her ideas & her writing

gaps in learning:
- application of reading, writing, speaking strategies in her other classes.

risks which resulted in development:
- extending the length of presentation & experimenting with format when speaking to the class
- incorporating details from personal observation logs into her writing

Goals for summer and the fall semester:
- making personal connections as she reads over the summer as a way of interacting with the text & as a way of generating writing topics.

Figure 6-7.

touched each of the other learners' lives. The exchanges that have taken place, the observations that are made, and the perceptions that have changed affect the way in which classmates read and respond to the portfolios of others in the learning community. One such observation was made by Lisa, who responded to Mike's portfolio when his reflections indicated that he hadn't seen very much development in his ability to speak with others in the class. Lisa wrote that she disagreed with his analysis. At the beginning of the year, he always sat by himself next to the window in the corner of the room, but by midyear he was joining the circle without being invited, and he now volunteered his ideas without being asked.

When each class shares with all other classes, an authentic audience of readers engages in the text of an author they don't know. These written responses are based solely on the text that was provided and artifacts that are displayed. Authors are given feedback not only on their learning, but on how well they considered their audience by providing background information and an analysis that is complete enough so that readers don't have to make too many assumptions. When readers are perplexed with a portfolio that has made too many assumptions, they gain valuable information that will help them write their reflective self-evaluations in their next portfolios.

By sharing with other students, authors of portfolios gain confirmation, applause, and suggestions for moving their learning forward from an audience of peers whose opinion the adolescent holds in high regard. Both the author and the reader can begin to plan for their next portfolio experience by observing the variety of formats and techniques used to assemble artifacts and written reflections on learning. As learners, they can also gain ideas for writing topics, ways to respond to literature, strategies, insights for analysis in self-evaluation, and suggestions for books to read.

The following responses, shown in Figure 6-8, found at the end of Lisa's portfolio demonstrate the connections learners can make between their own learning and those of another classmate. These connections can then be applied to future experiences in reading, writing, and the portfolio process.

The Family

How much responsibility parents should have in their child's learning is an excellent topic for discussion with the older student. As much as we would like a simple answer to that question, it's just not there when each student's story is considered. For some of our students who are seventeen, eighteen, and nineteen years old, there is a strong belief that they should have broken parental ties by this time and, in many cases, they are struggling to do so. Other students have parents who want to be involved in their child's education, but they don't know how or to what degree it is appropriate now that the student is growing towards independence. Still other students say that it is an older brother or sister who takes most of the responsibility for them, especially in bilingual homes where the parents haven't had the opportunity to learn English, but the older siblings have as a result of their schooling.

Much of our students' hesitation to share with parents was initially based on a concern one student finally vocalized. Many of the personal experiences he had chosen for writing topics were experiences about which he

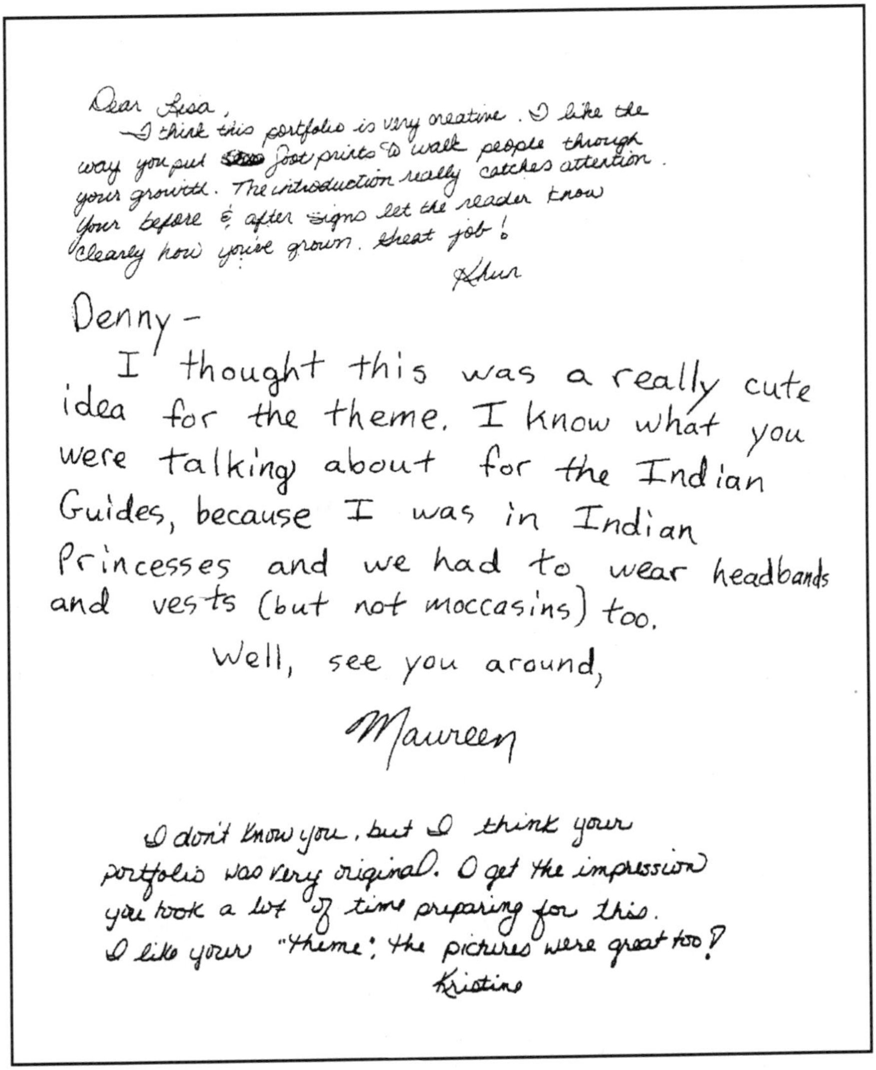

Dear Lisa,
   I think this portfolio is very creative. I like the way you put sticky foot prints to walk people through your growth. The introduction really catches attention. Your before & after signs let the reader know clearly how you've grown. Great job!
                         Ken

Denny –
   I thought this was a really cute idea for the theme. I know what you were talking about for the Indian Guides, because I was in Indian Princesses and we had to wear headbands and vests (but not moccasins) too.
     Well, see you around,

         Maureen

   I don't know you, but I think your portfolio was very original. I get the impression you took a lot of time preparing for this. I like your "theme": the pictures were great too!
               Kristine

Figure 6-8.

hadn't told his parents. For him, some of the most meaningful pieces of writing for purposes of analyzing his development as a writer dealt with topics he was not comfortable sharing with his parents. Since that time, students facing the same dilemma have revised their portfolio by using a three-ring binder to add or remove portions depending on the intended audience.

Family members who read the portfolio have the opportunity to see what the learner thinks through writing that is displayed, reactions to literature, and analysis of their process. Further, readers of portfolios are provided with information that can be used to support learners in their endeavors to meet future goals. An understanding of the learning experiences in the classroom is also gained, which can provide support for our instructional methods that are new and many times confusing to parents.

School Personnel

It was not surprising to learn from our students that other teachers, instructional aides, counselors, coaches, and the school principal were people they considered as possible audiences for their portfolios. The team effort in working with the whole student, not just the English student, athlete, or the one with a behavior problem is one of the most positive aspects of our school system. We knew that our students' portfolios had the potential to help other school personnel understand what was going on in our classrooms and to see the development of our students. With their portfolios, our students opened the door to discussions and questions about how they learn and what the implications might be for instruction not only between themselves and the person with whom they shared, but eventually the portfolio may also open a door between colleagues and ourselves. Another teacher can read the portfolios of students in a nonthreatening way and learn about an individual's processes, the content of the class, and the instruction that took place in the classroom.

Next we asked the students to consider who in the school has an influence on and takes some responsibility for their learning. The list grew to include the superintendent, the business manager, secretaries, school board members, and janitors. These people influence the curriculum, supplies and materials, and classroom arrangements. For example, after reading several portfolios, the business manager had a new understanding of learning. As a result, the complaints about the arrangements of desks, chairs, and tables in our classrooms made by the janitor assigned to our wing of the building were put to a halt.

Over the past three years, our teaching situation has changed dramatically, and we attribute this in part to our students who have shared their portfolios with school personnel. This year all freshman English classes were detracked and the curriculum was rewritten. Even the textbook approval form that needed to be filled out for board approval had to be rewritten to include literature other than the short stories found in a basal text. The novels that were chosen for the core curriculum were not compared to the novels that other schools were using nor were they chosen because of a readability level, which were considerations in the past. And since we no longer look at portfolios as an assessment tool, we are now researching various forms of alternative assessments. We believe that the freedom we gained to experiment with and make decisions related to curriculum was facilitated by portfolio sharing.

Important Others

Neighbors, friends, coworkers, bosses, relatives, and youth ministers have read and written responses in our students' portfolios. These are the people who have requested additional books to read with our students and then have held discussions over the phone or around a kitchen table. Most importantly, these people represent the support, usually in the form of encouragement, that our students need. Like their classmates these are the people who can applaud the development of the learner and show they are proud of the risks that were taken. The goals that students set and recorded in their portfolios have been supported and encouraged by these people.

Portfolio Visitors

When new students enter our classroom, we face the overwhelming task of explaining how our classroom functions as well as expanding the community to include these new members, who also need to get to know the other members. By giving these students several portfolios to read, they can begin to learn about the materials we read, our strategies for making meaning of literature, the types of writing we have completed and our process for revision, the role and expectations of the teacher, and the values of the learning community. We then ask several of the authors of these portfolios to spend a class period talking with these new students about their portfolios and answering any questions they might have. Our students are then responsible for introducing new members to the rest of the class.

Whenever we speak at conferences or are invited to work with teachers during staff development sessions at their schools, we take a stack of student portfolios with us. Our students are always anxious to hear what another educator has to say about their learning and their creation. The students who have authored these portfolios receive feedback from an authentic audience who isn't personally connected and whose response is based solely on the artifacts and text that are presented as seen in Figure 6-9.

Deeana's question (see Figure 6-1) pushed us to experiment with the various audiences who might respond to a student's portfolio and, from this experimentation, we began to see that the portfolio could and should mark the beginning of new learning experiences. Prior to that time, when we were using portfolios as an alternative assessment instrument, they were returned to the students' file folders once we had read them. Like the traditional final exam, they became symbolic of "the end" of learning. As learners and educators, we know that one learning experience is not sepa-

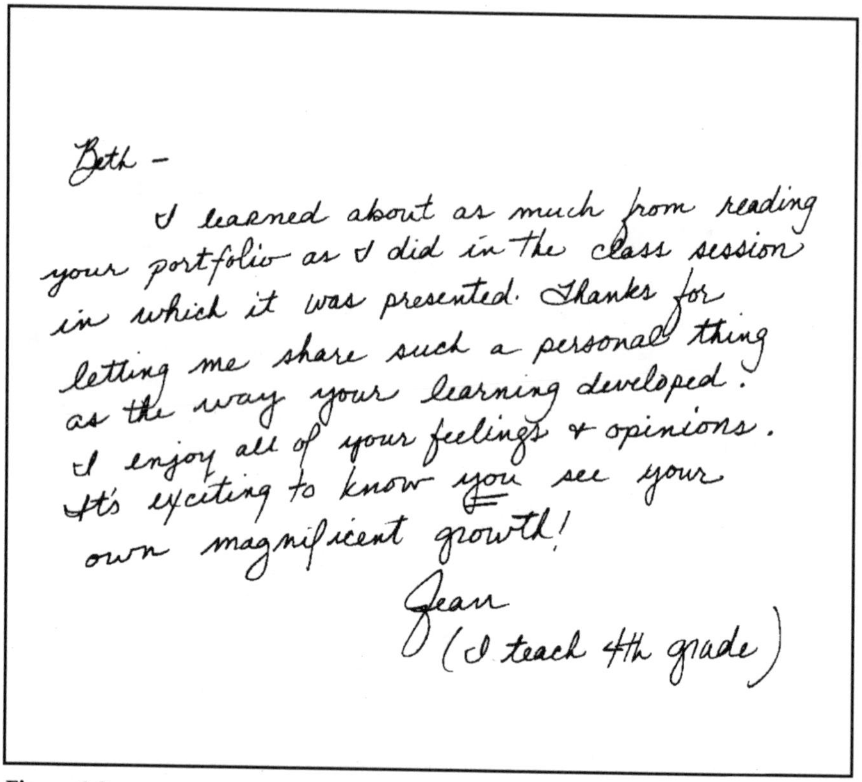

Beth –

    I learned about as much from reading your portfolio as I did in the class session in which it was presented. Thanks for letting me share such a personal thing as the way your learning developed. I enjoy all of your feelings & opinions. It's exciting to know you see your own magnificent growth!

               Jean
               (I teach 4th grade)

Figure 6-9.

rate and distinct from subsequent ones. There is a link between the known and the new. After completing a piece of writing, the writer will not approach the next piece in exactly the same way because that writer is not the same person who completed the previous piece. Closing the cover of a book after reading the final page does not mean that the reader's mind has closed when the next engagement in reading takes place. It is not unusual for readers to pick up another novel by an author they have previously read or one that approaches a similar topic in a different way. Other reading choices may be made by their potential to answer a question that grew from a previous experience. When the portfolio has been used as a learning strategy, a portion of the self-evaluation process is to determine what needs to be done next. The answer to that question becomes the bridge between the learner's past and future experiences.

    The portfolio can serve as the blueprint that will guide the learner, with the help of the teacher, in their literature choices; topics, formats, and experimentation with writing; and strategies to enhance learning. The ways in which we move the learning forward after goals are identified in the portfolio have become still another area of experimentation. Since we value and work toward students accepting responsibility for their own learning, we want to hold them accountable for the goals they have set. However, as facilitator of the learning, we need to work with students to help them achieve their goals.

Although conferences are the most time-consuming method of coming to a shared understanding of the goals that students establish after the reflective process of portfolios, we still find that it is the most effective method. Because of the amount of writing that takes place with reflective narratives in the portfolio, shortly after the portfolio has been completed is a good time for students to settle in with a new book. It is also an excellent time to schedule conferences with students. Having learned from our past mistakes, we have also found that a more efficient use of time is gained if students prepare for the conference by thinking of questions they have for us and determining steps they might take to meet their goals. This approach further shifts the responsibility and ownership of the goals to the learner.

Even though we try to set time limits for these conferences, we always seem to need to schedule some students before or after school, or during our planning and supervisory time (see Figure 6-10).

Any method of identifying, in simple terms, the goals students have set for themselves is helpful. A written document listing the student's goals serves a purpose similar to a grocery list containing the different items that need to be purchased from the store. Usually once the items needed are written down, they are remembered. Goal sheets work in much the same way—once goals are committed to paper, they are remembered. But just as we tuck that grocery list into our purse or pocket and pull it out when we seem lost in the aisles, so too can students use their goal sheets. These can refresh their memory when they get caught up in the learning and forget the overall direction in which they were heading, or are completing an event to make sure they didn't forget the underlying purpose that was guiding their experience. Students in one of Janell's classes began to staple these sheets, an example of which is shown in Figure 6-11, to their learning folders as a way to remind themselves of their goals on a regular basis.

From time to time our students step back from their engagements in learning to reflect on how successful they have been in attempting to achieve their goals. This might be at the end of the day, week, unit, etc. Ongoing reflection can help students assess how well and to what degree goals have been met. With this determination the things that helped them achieve their goals or that possibly stood in the way of their achievement can be analyzed. If needed, new goals can be set or those that were too general can be made more specific.

Often, students discover other needs they have to satisfy as learners before they can accomplish their larger goal. One student, for example, set

Figure 6-10.

a goal to contribute at least one idea to literature discussion each time his group met. When he was unable to meet this goal, Carol discovered that he was only making personal connections and writing summaries in his written responses to literature. Once he was able to write questions in response to his reading, he was then able to ask questions during literature discussion. These reflections can be written on the goal sheet itself, in a letter to the teacher, or by answering the reflective questions, "What have I done?" "What am I doing?" "Why did I change?" "What remains to be done?" In order to support students as they search for ways to accomplish their goals, we need to explore the following questions:

- As a learning strategy, how much time should there be between portfolios?

- How can we continue to keep students focused on their goals?

- How can students use information from previous portfolios to support their current understanding?

GOALS FOR _Michelle_

DATE _September   - October_

READING: keep working to think about how I am reading and reminds myself of places and people that I know.

WRITING: as I freewrite, keep asking myself questions such as who? what? where? how did I feel? and why? That will help me with details

I showed the most improvement in clustering (they got bigger. because I understood the consept better. and writing because I was giving more details.

Most effective reading strategy:
written conversation because I could tell the person how I felt and ask them questions then they could give me answers back.

Most effective writing strategy:
freewrites because they're about me - things that have happened that I know.

Figure 6-11.

Lyndi
Age 10

Andi
Age 3

DURING THE COURSE of our experimentation, there was a change in administration and our parental support continued to grow, which enabled us to experiment and take risks more openly than we could have if we had been in a more traditional school environment. This freedom and our collaboration allowed us to move forward quickly, and locally we became known as pioneers in the area of alternative assessment. Each year the invitations to speak at teacher in-services and at local, state, and national conferences increased. We originally spoke as a team, but in order to reach a wider audience, we now speak separately, drawing in other members of our department to share their expertise. Regardless of the audience, we have found some questions to be universal. Too often it appears that, without the answers to these questions, teachers are reluctant to implement change even though, philosophically, they agree with the concept of portfolios as a learning strategy. We want to share those questions and our tentative answers in order to support teachers as they take risks, and we want to allow them to benefit from our "errors" and subsequent revisions.

WHAT IF THE PORTFOLIO AUDIENCE DOESN'T APPRECIATE THE DEVELOPMENT OF THE LEARNER?

When the reader of the portfolio values the correct use of language more than the development of the learner, the teacher may have to face this problem. As learners, we know from experience that correctness and development do not happen simultaneously. We also know from experience that mistakes can be valuable learning experiences. When this concern has been brought to our attention by someone who has read one of our student's portfolios, we explain that our purpose in having students reflect on their learning is a way for them to gain a deeper understanding of their learning process. We could require that journal entries be edited, for example, but we doubt that most students would search for understanding or consider spur of the moment ideas if we required them to edit. Our students do share their reflective narratives with classmates for feedback and proofreading suggestions, since they are written for an audience. However, as teachers and students, we keep our purpose of using the portfolio as a learning strategy in mind as we determine to what extent the narratives should be edited.

Our parents and administration have always appreciated the development of our students when the portfolio was shared with them. We take advantage of every opportunity to inform these two audiences about our understanding of the learning process and how this translates into classroom practices. We provide articles to the administrators and write a brief description of how the article influenced our approach to instruction. We write letters to the parents and share articles with them as often as possible.

Open house and progress-report time are also valuable opportunities to share not only what we are doing in the classroom, but what we have learned from our students. For every piece of information sent home to parents, a sample copy is provided to our administrators. An example of one such correspondence, shown in Figure 7-1, is a goal letter written during a student and teacher conference.

These goal letters document not only what a student is able to do well, but help the student and teacher together determine what needs to be done next. Subsequent learning experiences require students to work toward achieving their goal. With each new assessment, the student and teacher will determine if the goal has been met. This determination is supported by evaluating the degree of progress toward achieving the goal. Throughout the semester, we view the final product as one portion of the student's learning process, but it is not the ultimate goal. Goals are beyond the student's immediate grasp. They require risk-taking on the part of the learner. If perfection in a final product is the only goal, students will not take the necessary risks to expand their current capabilities. The final product is valued, but it does not interfere with learning along the way.

Each time an assessment is made and new goals are set, a letter is mailed home. By the time parents read their students' portfolios, a minimum of four letters have been mailed and parent-teacher conferences and open house sessions have taken place. The letter shown in Figure 7-2 accompanied the portfolios of our students the first time we asked for parental response. Today the letter and appropriate articles such as "New Report Cards Portfolios Are Changing the Way Kids Get Graded" (Thomas 1992, 34-37) are optional, if the student decides the audience may need these for better understanding.

In order for readers to appreciate the development of the learner, they must be able to see the differences between early engagements in learning and those that were created later. If students show one of their first pieces of writing, for example, alongside some of their most recent samples, their development can be showcased. Just placing the pieces side by side isn't enough. The reflective narrative needs to provide an analysis of the changes that have occurred from one engagement to the next. Unless students have had experience in looking back at their learning this will not be an easy task. We have found that if students work with a partner, the unbiased "eye" of the other person is more likely to notice the differences between pieces of writing than the writer who is too closely tied to the artifact. Brainstorming a list of developmental changes that classmates have noted will also give students a direction for investigation. Finally, we also have students go back to their goal sheets for a reminder of the specific skills they had been working on at the time when the piece was created. This way, they can use their reflective narratives to describe what their area of focus was and to determine if they accomplished their goals.

Last week I asked Oscar to assess his learning over the past 41/2 weeks asking: where was I as a reader, writer, speaker and listener; and, where am I now? We looked back at the strategies we had used to improve writing and reading comprehension. Our conference indicated that some positive steps have been made in learning. We have set goals and identified ways that these goals might be attained by Oscar . A brief summary of our conference follows. Please discuss it with Oscar and if you have any questions please feel free to call me

Reading
Area of Growth:

Responses to reading are becoming more extended and show that Oscar searching
Goal: *for understanding of the text.*

To ask questions and explore possible answers

Step(s):

1. *Use bookmarks to record questions.*
2. *Guess at some possible answers.*
Writing   3. *Share questions with discussion group.*
Area of Growth: 4. *Consider revisions to your original ideas*

Adding visual details to writing.
Goal:

To add variety to sentence structure

Step(s) to Meet Goal:

1. *Proofread beginnings of sentences with an "eye" for repetition of words.*
2. *Read pieces aloud and listen for structures in sentences that sound the same.*

Figure 7-1.

WHAT IF MY SCHOOL DISTRICT REQUIRES THAT I GRADE MY STUDENTS' PORTFOLIOS?

We have learned that the portfolio should be a collaborative process between the students and teacher. If students have determined with their teacher how the portfolio can support their learning, they should also have input on how a portfolio should be graded. For instance, students have decided that each artifact needs to be introduced to the reader, who needs to know what the item is and why it was chosen. When we ask students how

Speaking
Area of Growth:

> *Beginning to share his ideas concerning the novel we are reading.*

Goal:

> *To become more comfortable with speaking in front of classmates*

Step(s) to Meet goal:

> *1 Determine questions and predictions prior to discussion by considering these while writing bookmarks*

Listening
Area of Growth:

> *Listens to the ideas of others*

Goal:

> *To determine how the ideas of classmates alter his understanding of literature.*

Step(s) to meet Goal:

> *1. Formulate "guesses" in relation to your questions about literature.*
> *2 Reflect in writing on how you changed your interpretations based upon the ideas of others*

Figure 7-1 cont'd.

their portfolios should be graded, they state that introductions should be eval-
uated for a portion of their grade. If teachers invite students to be a part of
the process, and we believe they should, then teachers shouldn't exclude students from being a part of forming an evaluation instrument. We develop
evaluation instruments collaboratively with our students. Each form that we
use is unique to each class that we teach (see Figures 7-3 and 7-4.) For this reason, we encourage our readers to follow the same advice with evaluation
forms as we offered with beginning portfolios: find a place to start, even if
you make a few mistakes (p. 1). Developing the evaluation instrument collaboratively with students is a valuable learning experience.

Dear Parents:

Less than a year ago the reading/writing lab was only in the planning stages. We (the teachers) had some dreams of what the program could be for the students. Our expectations for each student were that they would come to value, appreciate, and learn from their reading, writing, listening, and speaking. Many students read their first novel this year, some have finally broken the one page barrier in writing, and student discussions are no longer a fearful time, but rather a time to value each voice in the classroom.

As our final learning experience this year, we have asked the students to compile their work into a portfolio. Portfolios are a way of displaying what a person can do. It is our belief that they can also represent how much a person has learned. This is why we also use the portfolio as a final exam. Your child will be answering a series of questions reflecting on his/her learning this past year/semester. Since we feel strongly that contact with parents is an integral part of each student's success, we hope you will enjoy their portfolio with them. Please take the time to respond to the questions on the following page. You can send your response to us through your child.

Please do not hesitate to call us   or to write a note at the bottom of the survey if you have any questions and/or suggestions concerning your child's progress or next year's program.

We hope as our students look back to this school year, they will have many memorable learning experiences that will guide and assist them in their future coursework and careers.

Sincerely,

Carol Porter
Janell Cleland
Chapter I Teachers

Figure 7-2.

WHAT SHOULD BE DONE WITH THE PORTFOLIO AT THE END OF THE SCHOOL YEAR?

Portfolios that have been created for accountability or assessment have generally stayed in a filing cabinet long after students complete their coursework or graduate. The underlying purpose of this type of portfolio is to document material that was covered by the teacher and to record the end products used to assess the degree to which a student learned. At one time, we kept our students' portfolios as a way to revisit where students were and what we needed to do as teachers to support their learning. At the end of

```
                          Portfolio Grading Sheet

 Yes  No  1. Is the portfolio neat in appearance?


 Yes  No  2. Does the portfolio inform a general audience about the learner you
             were and the learner you've become?


          3. For each artifact in your portfolio have you explained:
 Yes  No     Where you were in your learning before you wrote the piece,
             read the book etc., shared your ideas, or listened to others?


 Yes  No     Where you are now in your learning as a result of the writing,
             reading, speaking, or listening to others?


 Yes  No     What you learned that is represented by the artifact?


 Yes  No  4. Have you drawn the reader (audience) into the portfolio by being
             original, creative, and/or imaginative?


          5. Have you displayed learning in each of the following areas:
 Yes  No     Reading


 Yes  No     Writing


 Yes  No     Speaking


 Yes  No     Listening
```

Figure 7-3.

the school year, we boxed up a portion of our students' lives and placed them on the shelf in the corner of our room. From time to time we would go back to these portfolios when we had an instructional question or when we needed samples for our new students as they began the portfolio process. But the mother in each of us felt a guilty tug. We asked ourselves, "If our children had put together similar stories of their lives, would we want their

---

Grade Sheet for The Writing Portfolio

_____ 10   Does the reader of the portfolio get a sense of the writer you were at the beginning of the semester?
* Introduction to your attitude toward writing, strengths as a writer, weaknesses as a writer. . .

_____ 10   Does the portfolio highlight your strengths as a writer?
* In the written text
* Supported with artifacts (examples from your work)

_____ 10   Does the portfolio identify the weaknesses you still have as a writer?
* In the written text
* Supported with artifacts
(What is left to be done if you are to become a better writer?)

_____ 10   Does the portfolio identify the goals you set for yourself as a writer over the semester?
* In the written text
* Supported with artifacts
(What did you try to accomplish? Which goals did you accomplish? Which goals weren't accomplished?)

_____ 10   Does the reader understand why each artifact was chosen to be included in the portfolio?
* In the written text
(Why is the piece meaningful to you as a writer?)

_____ 10   Does the portfolio summarize and/or draw conclusions about your changes and/or lack of change and set goals for future learning experiences?
* In the written text
(Overall, how are you the same writer? How are you a different writer? What have you learned that will help you in future learning situations?)

_____ 10   Does the portfolio describe what caused the changes (or the lack of change) that occurred (or didn't occur)?
* In the written text
* Supported with artifacts
(Strategies that helped, Attitude/ideas about writing, Instruction, Classmates, Computer. . .)

_____ 10   Has your portfolio been shared with someone else for a response?

_____ 10   Creativity/Originality

_____ 10   Neatness

Figure 7-4.

teachers to box them up and put them in a corner of their room?" Of course not. These stories belong to their authors. The answer to that question was probably the simplest one we have had to answer since embarking on our experimentation with portfolios.

When the portfolio is used as a learning strategy, the purpose is to enhance individual process awareness and promote goal setting. Our students go back to their previous portfolio(s) each time they begin a new one. Some students continue in their old portfolio and simply add a new chapter.

However, when a prior portfolio is not connected to the reflections in the new portfolio, it should be given to the student to take home. If there is a continuity of philosophy from teacher to teacher, keeping the students' portfolio at the end of the year may be appropriate.

Photocopying the portfolio is one way a copy can remain in the classroom if the teacher has a reason for keeping it. As we write this book, we are experimenting with scanning portfolios and storing them on a computer disk. In this way students can access documents from an earlier period of time or other classes and analyze development over longer periods of time. The still video has allowed students to take pictures of each artifact and tell the story of their learning orally. This camera has also been useful for catching students' learning behaviors as they are engaged in reading, writing, and discussion. We believe that technology will eventually make this question easier to answer and create possibilities for portfolios that we may not have imagined. In the meantime record keeping by the teacher can be time consuming and complex, but if anecdotal records (Goodman 1989, 10) and goal sheets (Chapter 6) have been kept all along, the information gained can be added to the teacher's other system(s) of documentation and the portfolio can remain with its rightful owner.

WHEN SHOULD THE PORTFOLIO BE USED AS A LEARNING STRATEGY?

One of our most recent uses for the portfolio came as a result of detracking our freshman English classes. During our initial curriculum meetings, we discussed the characteristics of effective curriculum and instruction. These discussions eventually led to setting the curricular goals shown in Figure 7-5. But how could we assess these goals within our current traditional grading system that required a nine-weeks grade? Denny Wolfe eloquently voiced a similar concern: "When student writers focus on the end product — which turns out to be not so much the paper, but the grade — they lose interest in the process. Worse, they take very few risks with their writing." (1986, 1) This was exactly what we hoped to avoid within our new program. Jodi Wirt, an active member of the curriculum team, joined Janell to explore assessment alternatives that addressed these concerns, and their discussions led to experimentation with a learning portfolio.

One component of our new curriculum consisted of teaching core reading and writing strategies. The core strategies for the first grading period included free writing, written conversation, clustering, and most important word. Throughout the first three weeks, the students experimented with these strategies as we read short stories and poetry. During class, we discussed the

Freshman English

Course Goals ¡

1.0 Students are discovering their own learning process through language experiences by
   1.1 identifying various purposes for communication.
   1.2 exploring ways to generate ideas.
   1.3 experimenting with a variety of learning strategies.
   1.4 identifying learning strategies that are most effective in supporting their learning.

2.0 Students are valuing collaboration through the sharing of work, discussing of ideas and reaching a common goal by
   2.1 modeling attitudes and behaviors of an effective group member.
   2.2 providing effective feedback to peers during a shared writing or literature discussion.
   2.3 identifying purposes for and advantages associated with collaboration.
   2.4 demonstrating an appreciation of differences in opinions.

3.0 Students are developing critical thinking and problem solving skills through language experiences by
   3.1 engaging in active and purposeful inquiry to expand their knowledge.
   3.2 generating questions and predictions and giving rationales before, during, and after a variety of language experiences.
   3.3 drawing inferences appropriate to achieving a full understanding of the text.
   3.4 using specific information or reasons to support personal interpretations of language experiences.
   3.5 integrating information from print and non-print sources.
   3.6 understanding that inquiry is an integral part of the learning process.
   3.7 identifying, planning, and executing individual projects.
   3.8 applying criteria to support personal evaluation of literature.

4.0 Students are discovering the characteristics of effective communication by
   4.1 generating and presenting one's original thoughts and ideas.
   4.2 understanding and evaluating the ideas of others orally and in writing
   4.3 using appropriate language and style in communicating for a specific purpose and audience.
   4.4 analyzing and critiquing other's ideas when presented orally or in writing.
   4.5 developing and maintaining a focus using specific information or reasons to support and elaborate the thesis or main point.
   4.6 organizing ideas clearly, concisely, and logically for the appropriate format.
   4.7 using standard written English conventions.
   4.8 incorporating revision and editing strategies.

Figure 7-5.

qualities of effective written conversation, free writing, and other strategies and shared not only our own entries but entries from previous students and from class volunteers. We focused on improving each renewed attempt at a strategy and felt that each strategy should be used a minimum of three times to effectively determine how well it was working for that student. We also requested that the students apply one of the strategies of their choice in one of their other classes and that they should be prepared to discuss why it did or didn't work. At the end of the three weeks, students compiled their work by first to most recent use of a strategy. This collection became a learning portfolio, since we asked the students to reflect on what they had learned about themselves as readers and writers as a result of trying these new strategies. Since few of our students had any experience with self-reflection, we provided the questions shown in Figure 7-6 to assist them as they examined the work in their portfolio.

Our purpose was to allow the students to see their own growth as readers and writers and to gain a new understanding of their learning process. We realized the danger of trying to affix a grade to a student's growth and learning process. We also realized that we needed to determine a number to put in the grade book, since nine-weeks grades and grade-point averages are still a reality within our current system. We shared these concerns with our students and with their input we devised the grade sheet shown in Figure 7-7.

We did not ask the students to choose their most meaningful artifact from the first three weeks, but rather to make sense of what they had done by examining all their work to that point. The grade sheet reflected this shift by including points for quantity (having completed all the required strategies); however, we felt that quantity should only be a factor early in the year, as new freshmen were learning to stay organized and learning to keep track of all their papers. In subsequent grade sheets, quantity would change to quality, and students received points for incorporating qualities of an effective response into their own writing. Certainly there is a grade involved in the use of a portfolio, but the message is clear that it is the growth and understanding of one's personal learning process that results in that grade.

At this point we were ready to begin our first novel, *The Acorn People* by Ron Jones. The core reading strategy for the novel was bookmarks (Chapter 4), and with our students we determined seven points in the reading where we would stop and record on our bookmarks reactions to what we had read. After the first four responses, we color-coded our bookmarks (Chapter 4) and set personal reading goals for our final three bookmarks. Once again, the students compiled all of their bookmarks in chronological order and closed their portfolio with a reflective letter to us that focused on their growth and understanding of process. We also asked them to set goals for future responses to literature.

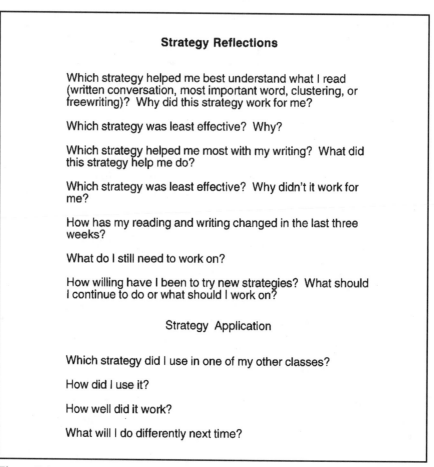

Strategy Reflections

Which strategy helped me best understand what I read (written conversation, most important word, clustering, or freewriting)? Why did this strategy work for me?

Which strategy was least effective? Why?

Which strategy helped me most with my writing? What did this strategy help me do?

Which strategy was least effective? Why didn't it work for me?

How has my reading and writing changed in the last three weeks?

What do I still need to work on?

How willing have I been to try new strategies? What should I continue to do or what should I work on?

Strategy Application

Which strategy did I use in one of my other classes?

How did I use it?

How well did it work?

What will I do differently next time?

Figure 7-6.

Michelle's portfolio, shown in Figures 7-8, 7-9, and 7-10, provides an example of a student who used the portfolio as a strategy to improve her responses to literature and to heighten her awareness of her learning process. She also gained valuable experience in reflective thinking.

The grade sheet for *The Acorn People* (see Figure 7-11) provides a space where the students record their reading goals. It also shows how we incorporated the quality component into the grade and shows our continued focus on applying the core strategy in other areas.

Although we are constantly revising our efforts, we believe we have successfully devised an instrument that supports our beliefs about learning while allowing students to experience success in a way that encourages them to take risks and, therefore, improve the quality of their reading and writing. At the same time, we were able to address the common concerns

```
                        FRESHMEN ENGLISH
                        LEARNING PORTFOLIO

QUANTITY - 12 ENTRIES  = 5
           10,11       = 4
            8, 9       = 3
            6, 7       = 2
            4, 5       = 1          1  2  3  4  5  x2 = _____

GROWTH
            1.  Do freewrites show evidence of extended writing
                time and greater detail?    Yes    No
            2.  Do written conversations display a more genuine
                understanding of the literature?    Yes    No
            3.  Are more connections being made between personal
                experience and language experiences?   Yes    No
            4.  Is there evidence that the student is taking more
                risks?   Yes    No
            5.  Is there demonstrated evidence that the student is
                a contributing member of the class community?

                               1  2  3  4  5  x4 = _____


REFLECTION
            1.  Does the learner determine which strategy best
                supported his/her learning?    Yes    No
            2.  Does the learner determine which strategy was
                least effective?    Yes    No
            3.  Are answers supported with specific references
                to the strategy displayed in the portfolio?
                Yes    No
            4.  Does the learner determine how his/her reading and
                writing have changed in the last three weeks?
                Yes    No
            5.  Have realistic goals been set with a plan of
                action?   Yes    No
                               1  2  3  4  5  x2 = _____


APPLICATION
            Each question answered with satisfactory detail
               and evidence of strategy = 5
            3 answers and strategy      = 4
            2 answers and strategy      = 3
            1 answer and strategy       = 2

                               1  2  3  4  5  x2 = _____

Total possible = 50 points
                    45 - 50 = A
                    40 - 44 = B
                    35 - 39 = C
                    30 - 34 = D          Your total is _____
```

Figure 7-7.

that accompany detracking by focusing on the development of each learner
by setting and monitoring individual reading and writing goals.

BEYOND READING AND WRITING, HOW MIGHT THE PORTFOLIO BE USED AS A LEARNING STRATEGY?

Whenever we are involved in learning, reflexivity is a part of the process.
This is often an unconscious part. The portfolio helps to bring what we have

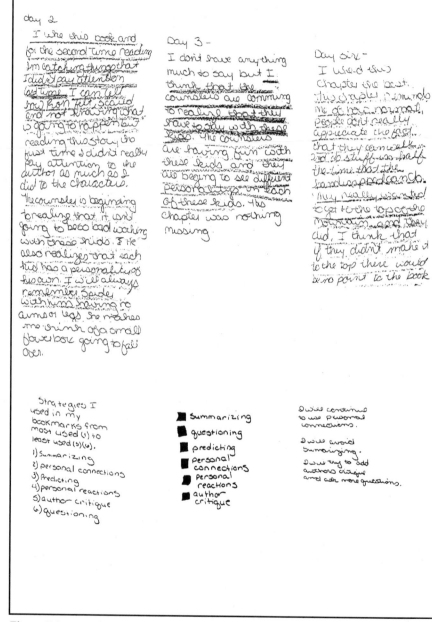

Figure 7-8.

Day 7, 8, 10 –
Michelle
These three chapters
made me think of
how much fun these
kids had. This rem-
inded me of when
there was a pancake
breakfast at my
brothers school. There
were these down
Syndrome people
at this table. I was
assigned to help that
table. After awhile
they started to call
me by name. Then
this one guy kissed
my hand and all
of the people clapped
so I patted him on
the head. You never
saw a bigger smile.

3 to 0 days left –
I think that the
water show is a good
idea. I hope they
get to do it the way
they want to. This
reminds me of when
I went to a basketball
Camp and you got to
make skits! It
was fun but we
didn't know what
to do because we
thought we might
look stupid.

Day 8 –   Michelle
I think they labeled
everything because
they wanted the parents
to know they were
doing educational
stuff.

She wanted them
to act the way they
normally do because
that is what makes them
neat.

they were labeling
them for what they
were but not who they
are.

that they weren't really
being their selves.
Once the labels went
off they were back to
their old self.

0 days left + Epilog –
I liked the water
show because the
kids really got to
show how they act.
I also thought that
was a good way to close
Camp because it made
everyone happy and
it would probably
be something that
they all would remember.
I wonder how long
Spider and Martin
would have lived
if they weren't in a
car accident.

Figure 7-9.

Dear Mrs. Cleland,

I would recomend that The Acorn People stay in the freshman English curriculum because as a freshman I felt the same way as the author did. I had to try something new, I was scared and I had to overcome new obstacles.

I think that good responses on your bookmark is when the reader uses personal conections and asks questions, I think that it is important to use personal connections because it allowed me to get more interested in the book. For example, I remember being scared of these men tally handicapped people at my brothers pancake breakfast and from reading the book I discovered that these people are special in ways that we haven't realized, It is also important to ask questions because if you don't ask that question you will always be wondering what the outcome could have been if something different happened. after reading the epilog I asked the question, "How long would spider have lived if he hadn't gotten in the car accident. If I were still summarizing I wouldn't have thought of my question.

In my first bookmarks, I did a lot of summarizing. If you look back to days 2, and 3 it is underelined in green crayon. If I continued to summarize I wouldn't know the meaning of the book, I would just have enjoyed the book.

                —Michelle

Figure 7-10.

FRESHMAN ENGLISH
WRITTEN RESPONSES TO LITERATURE

Reading Goal(s):

Yes No   Is there evidence that steps were taken to accomplish the goal?

1 2 3 4 5 x2= _____

QUALITY

Yes No   Are there a variety of responses to the text?

Yes No   Are responses supported with specific examples and/orreferences to the text?

Yes No   Is there evidence that the reader is exploring something he/she might not understand as a way of gaining meaning?

Yes No   Is there evidence that the reader's responses to the text are the result of thoughtful reflection?

1 2 3 4 5 x2= _____

GROWTH

Yes No   Do responses show evidence of extended writing time and greater detail?

Yes No   Do responses display a more genuine understanding of the literature?

Yes No   Is there evidence that student is using responses to make meaning of text?

Yes No   Is there evidence that the student is making a variety of responses to the text?

Yes No   Is there demonstrated evidence that the student is a contributing member of the class community?

1 2 3 4 5 x3= _____

REFLECTION

Yes No   Are answers supported with specific references to the strategy (strategies) displayed in the portfolio?

Yes No   Is growth documented with before and after examples?

Yes No   Have realistic goals been set and do they have a plan of action?

Yes No   Does the learner determine the reason why a strategy does/doesn't work?

Yes No   Is there evidence that the entry was a result of thoughtful reflection by the student?

1 2 3 4 5 x2= _____

APPLICATION

5   Each question answered with satisfactory detail and evidence of strategy.

4   Strategy and 4 answers

3   Strategy and 3 answers

2   Strategy and 2 answer

1   Strategy and 1 answer

1 2 3 4 5 x1= _____

Figure 7-11.

learned about learning to a conscious level. When returning home after a vacation, for example, our families talk about what we enjoyed the most, what was a disappointment, and what we would change if we ever visited that area again. The portfolio provides a format for reflective exploration in much the same way because it requires decisions that take reflection beyond the realm of reminiscence.

The wrestling coach, whom Janell once worked with, videotapes his wrestlers during practice and at meets from their freshman through senior years. He meets regularly with these athletes to determine their strengths, analyze their development, and set goals. This year the freshman English students in our school have their own video that will be used to capture literature discussions, authors' circles, presentations, speeches, debates, skits and other demonstrations of oral language that occur. These tapes, like the tapes of the wrestlers, will follow the students through their senior year and will be analyzed and used to set directions for student development.

One student we know is compiling an inquiry portfolio on the area of politics. His artifacts include reading materials and writing related to his learning. As a learning strategy, his portfolio also holds the information he has gained, new questions that have emerged, and the investigative processes explored. There are also products, demonstrations, and celebrations of his learning and the applications (both in knowledge and process) he is making to other learning situations.

For years, students in the performing arts have assembled portfolios that display what they can do, but as a learning strategy the portfolio can also help these students explore their process. One student in Carol's English class, who was known as one of the most talented artists in the school, was having difficulty getting started with his writing. He spent days agonizing over possible topics and interpreted his inability to decide as a writing deficiency. Finally, he used the portfolio as a strategy for choosing art work that best illustrated his development and then wrote a reflective narrative about his drawing process. As a result, he discovered that this process paralleled his writing process. He was then able to apply many of the same strategies to his writing that had been successful for him as an artist. (See Figures 7-12 and 7-13).

SHOULD I COMPILE A TEACHING PORTFOLIO? IF SO, HOW DO I BEGIN?

We have always read and written along with our students as a way to allow them to see the decisions we make in our own learning process. For one reason or another, it was over a year into using portfolios with our students that we actually began to share the experience with them by assembling our own.

Figure 7-12.

We followed our own advice and began to examine our learning and our teaching: what we had done, what we were doing, how we had changed, what we had learned, and what remained to be done.

Along with our students, we opened the folders where we also accumulated our own work throughout the semester. Frustration surfaced, and we realized how out of touch we had been with the concerns our students expressed when they couldn't decide which artifacts to choose. The list of possibilities seemed endless: our writing, our students' writing, photographs, process observations, pieces of meaningful literature, professional articles that had an impact on us. How could we narrow this mass to something manageable? The answer seemed to come in the form of another question: What is the purpose of my portfolio?

Janell decided to examine the principles that she used to guide decisions she made in the classroom. She included artifacts that would help her determine if she was successfully accomplishing those principles: community, risk-taking, demonstration, whole-to-part literacy, authenticity, choice, reflection, and process. Once her purpose was more clearly defined, she could return to "what needs to go in" and begin to make sense of her pile of artifacts. Next, she created a list of questions that she asked herself about

CHAP. I

The Dance

This was my first attempt to be a graphic artist. During a Inter Class Council meet of the Sr. Class, I was volunteered to create a poster for the winter dance (which the class was hosting). I thought it would be easy. Boy, was I wrong! All I thought I had to do is wip something on a Mac, and I'd be done. Easer said than done. First off the computer drafts were very ugly. Secondly, and most important, the printers were acting up. I just can't tape up disks every were, hoping that people just happen to have a portable computer on them.

Out of total frustration, I gave up, and went home for make one by hand. I went up stairs to my room, and sat down ready to wip up an awsome poster.

Figure 7-12 cont'd.

I sat there for an hour, staring at a blank sheet of paper. It was one of the worst "writers block" I've ever had.

This is not a story where our hero, all the sudden, gets a brilant idea, creates a master piece, and sells it for 2.5 million. No not so lucky. Our hero has writers block for 5 more days.

It is now Monday, deadline for the poster is Tuesday. The most I had was a scribble and a pile of paper wads. A lot of progress, huh? I finaly got insperation from a ~~littl~~ doodle I did in my A.P. Biology ~~note~~ note book. I was a drawing of a girl kissing a boy on the cheek. I went with it and 30 minutes later the finished product. It was the fastest I've ever put out a drawing. And at the time, one of my better desines.

The Next morning I gave the poster to Steve (our class president) and posters for the winter dance were made.

Figure 7-12 cont'd.

Figure 7-13.

The "Stress" of Running

Not to long ago T. J. Cintolo and Adam Andridsen had a music group (consisting of themselves). The songs they produced censided of keybords, electronic sounds, and Singing Vocals. To tell you the truth, they were pretty good, And very ambitious. So ambitious that they created a entire album. The album consisted of 8 songs, 2 of which were just instramental. They called the album "Stress Fracture". It is a term used for a hair line fracture in the bone from an abundance of Stress put on it (like running or jumping)

The part where I came in was when they needed a picture for the cover album. They asked me to do it for them. Of course I was happy to except. To make a long story short, they never got the drawing, nor did they ever finish an "album".

Figure 7-13 cont'd.

Two years later, while looking through my portfolio, I found my first draft. I thought it looked kind of neat, so I desided to redo it. It took me ~~far ever~~ forever to finish the drawing, almost a half a year. The reason for this is because of the large amounts of space that was dotted, or lined for texure.

The original draft was supposed to depict the word "stress fracture". When I had done ~~this I was~~ the first draft, I was in a creative Marathon. Things just kept popping out of my head. Some times, ~~when went~~ I'm creating a drawing, ~~It~~ it will be an ~~I~~ idea, a feeling, or just something that just looks right. It is very hard to explain. I guess you can call it artistic instinct.

This is my most interesting drawing so far. There is a lot of Symbolism, in it. None of which has anything to do with the definition of the word stress fracture. It is ~~based~~ based on the word "Stress". See if you can find all of it.

Figure 7-13 cont'd.

each of the areas she was exploring. For example, in the section where she explored her role as a demonstrator in the classroom, she asked herself the following questions:

What am I presently doing to demonstrate learning in my classroom?

What artifacts can I include in my portfolio that will reveal this?

What have I done throughout the semester?

What artifacts will reveal this?

How have I changed throughout the semester?

What have I learned?

What remains to be done in this area?

The answers to these questions helped her write the reflection on her classroom shown in Figure 7-14.

In Carol's first portfolio, she experimented with the format her students were using and developed a section for reading and for writing. In the entry, seen in Figure 7-15, Carol examined why a strategy that had previously been effective was no longer working in her Reading/Writing Lab.

Although we hadn't formally established teaching goals, we could see that our first portfolios were clearly organized around the goals that we had for our teaching and learning. The portfolios allowed us to examine those areas in a way that we seldom took the time to do. The examples we shared above illustrate that our portfolios mirrored the same purposes as the portfolios used by our students. We were able to examine how we valued process and how we took responsibility for our instructional decisions. We could see gaps in our learning, determine strategies that had been successful in the classroom, and see our changes and development over time. Finally, we celebrated risk-taking and inquiry and set future goals that might guide our next portfolios.

That is exactly what Carol did in her next portfolio, compiled during her first year as a department chairperson. She opened with the goals set for herself and then shared artifacts and reflections that showed the steps she had taken to accomplish those goals. (See Figure 7-16.)

This method of organizing the portfolios aligned with our growing belief that assessment should be a point where learning can be initiated rather than concluded, and we began to see the potential of using the portfolio for teacher evaluation procedures. Denny Wolfe defines evaluation during the writing process as "a process of seeking and receiving responses to one's writing for the purpose of revising" (1986, 2). When the focus is on revision rather than on judging the end product, evaluation can be viewed as instructional. If we accept that definition, then the portfolio can serve as the vehicle for seeking and receiving responses to one's teaching for the purpose of revision.

I began my teaching career as a speech and theater teacher, so demonstration always played an active role in my classroom. I loved to demonstrate all the different speeches for my students, and I was more than willing to fill in a scene when a student was absent. My own parents will attest to the fact that I have always loved to be on stage, and the classroom provided a daily captive audience. In those early teaching days I modeled what I thought to be the correct way to present oneself in front of an audience. I've grown to realize that it is much more effective to demonstrate one way, not the only way, that you might accomplish a certain task. In my speech classes one of the favorite speeches was the demonstration, and one piece of advice I gave to the demonstrators was to share any problems they might encounter while trying to accomplish the end product. Now I realize the importance of following that advice everyday in the classroom and showing students where I turn for answers when problems arise.

Last year I began sharing my writing with my students on a regular basis; this year I continued that practice. In April we began to read Romeo and Juliet in combination with a poetry unit. I suggested that my students might choose to try some poetry as their next piece of writing. Personally, I have never written a poem and still harbored a fear of even trying such a feat. This was the chance to push myself to the outer limits of demonstrating and risk-taking. I shared my first attempt at becoming a poet.

The whole demonstration began with a confession about my fear of even starting. This led to a discussion that lasted the entire class period. Students offered advice that former teachers had offered them, they shared similar feelings, or those who wrote poetry as a hobby "came out of the closet" and explained why they had always kept their love for

Figure 7-14.

writing poetry a secret. It was one of the most memorable days I had
with my freshmen last school year.

Still apprehensive about the whole idea, I turned to literature for
suggestions since that is where I find most of my writing topics. I had
always been draw to the Nurse while reading <u>Romeo and Juliet</u>, and while
reading late one evening, I suddenly realized why. The relationship
between the Nurse and Juliet reminded me of the bond that had existed
between my grandmother and myself. I was especially struck by the
frankness of the Nurse and Juliet's willingness to discuss her love for
Romeo. This reminded of evenings on my grandmother's front porch swing
when I would dump all my problems on her shoulders, and she would never
flinch even when I know I may have shocked her on occasion. I grabbed
the bookmarks which were intended for my reaction to the text and began
to jot down what I could remember most vividly about those evenings. I
was so excited by how quickly it was all happening that I wrote and
rewrote for over an hour. I couldn't wait to tell my students how it had
all happened, and they didn't disappoint me. They wanted to hear every
detail, and they encouraged me to try different formats with the final
draft. When we put together poetry portfolios later that month, many of
them asked me for a copy of my poem to include in their personal
favorites section. I can't begin to tell you how that made me feel.

Out of 64 students 58 of them decided to try their hand at poetry.
Even now as I look back I can't separate who was demonstrating for whom.
I think I started but then I think my students took over and guided me
through the process. It is one of the highlights of my school year!

Why do the girls
give me a hard time?

Why do boys chase
me home?

then on to college
the gone stayed the same

→ I got my first F.
my major is wrong.
Why don't boys
chase me home?

she seemed to know all
gave me the
answers I needed.

Figure 7-14 cont'd.

Porch Swing

Guess the color of passing cars
Red?
        Blue?
                Green?
Just an excuse
To sit on the swing
To share my thoughts
To ask my questions.
Time with the person
Who had the answers I needed.
My grandma invented the game.

Now I want a swing
A porch
A question.
Will my son want to play?
Red?
        Blue?
                Green?
I hope I remember
The rules
The answers.
I hope I can be so calm,
Unshaken.
I hope I remember her game.

(My students felt the jump
from childhood to parent was
too abrupt. My next draft
shows how I revised following
their suggestion.)

Figure 7-14 cont'd.

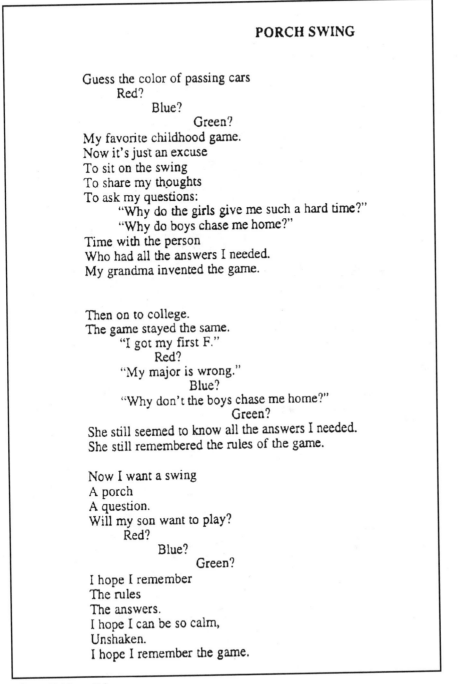

PORCH SWING

Guess the color of passing cars
    Red?
        Blue?
           Green?
My favorite childhood game.
Now it's just an excuse
To sit on the swing
To share my thoughts
To ask my questions:
    "Why do the girls give me such a hard time?"
    "Why do boys chase me home?"
Time with the person
Who had all the answers I needed.
My grandma invented the game.

Then on to college.
The game stayed the same.
    "I got my first F."
        Red?
    "My major is wrong."
           Blue?
    "Why don't the boys chase me home?"
             Green?
She still seemed to know all the answers I needed.
She still remembered the rules of the game.

Now I want a swing
A porch
A question.
Will my son want to play?
    Red?
        Blue?
           Green?
I hope I remember
The rules
The answers.
I hope I can be so calm,
Unshaken.
I hope I remember the game.

Figure 7-14 cont'd.

I made my first mistake when I let them choose from several other books that Duncan had written. They went off in so many directions that the support that helped them get through their first book no longer existed. Many were now writing bookmarks to a partner who wouldn't write back, and when is was time for them to discuss in their small groups, there were always several who hadn't read the material. The bookmarks that follow are shown as a contrast between two students who were ready to support each other in their reading and five who were not. Excitement dwindled, and the students returned to their famous excuse that the reason they hadn't finished the book was because it was boring.

These students were not ready
to support each other —
not because they didn't
Welcome- want to - it seems
Nuina   they didn't know how.
Rhonda
          Joe Larry

IT'S AN ODD BOOK I THINK I'VE
READ IT BEFORE
          LARRY

Larry - why do you think you have
read this before? why is it odd?
          Rhonder
I CAN'T DESCRIBE HOW IT'S ODD,
AND I THINK I'VE READ IT BEFORE
BECAUSE I HAVE. A CONDENSED VERSION
OF IT.

Laura- This book is good. if I were a nurse
and that happend to me I would freek rit.

Laura- This is a great book so far. I was
surprised to learn that Laura had a tattoo.
I wonder what she wants from Laura?

These 2 students were ready
to support each other with
their reading.

Laura,
          well I finally finished the
book. It is a very good book. I can't
believe it was Collie. I thought he
was a nice guy. I hated the ending
again I wanted to know what
all happen to them. thats all
I have to say.
                    MELISSA

I liked the ending I hope
that now the characters are
able to get over what they've
done. I wish Duncan had
said whether or not they
told the police everything
that happened. I can't
believe I didn't even suspect
Collie. Of course there was
no clue to help you guess
that Collie was Bud. oh well.
+ The Third Eye has a really
good ending I think you'll
like it.
          Laura

Figure 7-15.

I began this year with certain perceptions based upon my experiences and observations with the Communications Arts faculty over the past four years. I knew that shifting the focus regarding instruction was going to be difficult for everyone involved for a number of reasons.

- Many teachers were entrenched in their teaching style and felt threatened by the suggestion they change their beliefs about instruction.
- Many had suffered from a previous administration who had not viewed teachers as professionals and had used top-down leadership style. As a result, teachers were silenced in their efforts to have a voice in decision-making, particularly in the areas where their expertise should have been valued - curriculum and instruction.
- Most had been teaching in isolation. Collaboration and risk-taking were not valued.

After a summer of thinking, reading, taking classes, discussing, and formulating goals with these points in mind, I observed, read, thought, discussed and reformulated my goals during the first weeks of school. These are the goals that I currently have:

1. I want to demonstrate the variety of instructional methods that can be used during staff development time.
2. As much as possible I want to give teachers a voice in decision-making. I also want to show them that I will listen and I'm not "out to get them" by creating situations were their expertise is valued; particularly in the areas of curriculum and instruction.
3. I believe that divisional activities should promote collaboration so that risk-taking is not so threatening and teacher learning is not just reserved for beginning teachers.

Figure 7-16.

Similar to the student's portfolio, a teacher's portfolio might include artifacts that represent instructional strategies tried in the classroom, accompanied by reflections on the effectiveness of strategy. The final reflection might include future instructional goals that could be the starting point for the next portfolio. Evaluating these goals becomes instructional rather than judgmental, and teachers feel they have been involved in a collaborative effort. The goals for the next school year can be set before the teacher leaves for the summer, in case she wants to investigate possible strategies before returning in the fall. Unlike other evaluation instruments, this one provides an avenue for learning, just like the alternative assessment procedures we have devised for our classrooms. Wolfe also points out that "if our evaluating and grading procedures do not cause the student writers to write again, our procedures have failed" (1986, 2). This must also hold true for teacher evaluation instruments. If teachers no longer want to take risks and continue to learn because they fear the judgments that will be recorded in the personnel files, then the evaluation procedures have failed.

In closing this question and answer chapter, we want to encourage you not to let questions such as these pose roadblocks that keep you from experimenting in your classroom. Too often we speak at conferences where teachers seem to be looking for questions that will give them a reason to continue what has become routine for them. We have found questions to be our strategy for extending knowledge, not a convenient obstacle for standing still.

Our Final Reflections Chapter 8

Michelle

WHEN WE BEGAN to discuss how to conclude this book, those familiar feelings of uncertainty began to surface once again. We have read and reread the manuscript of this book well over one hundred times, and we are amazed that we are still struggling with portfolios and their implementation in each of our classrooms. How is it that two teachers who have written a book on portfolios can't seem to get it right? And if we still can't get it right after all this time, what type of encouragement is this to teachers who are considering their first attempts with portfolios or to those who want to approach them with a different focus?

It seemed like a monumental task to choose the right words to encourage teachers to explore the possibilities that portfolios might offer for themselves and their students. We want to ask our readers to assess where they are as they conclude this book, and then challenge them to set personal goals that will push them beyond their present level of understanding. This is exactly what our students do as they conclude each portfolio. We can provide, daily, the classroom environment where our students can take the type of risks that support their growth as learners, but how could we provide that type of encouragement and support in print to an audience we may never actually meet?

While searching for an answer to that question, we returned to our definition of portfolio:

> A collection of artifacts accompanied by a reflective narrative that not only helps the learner to understand and extend learning, but invites the reader of the portfolio to gain insight about learning and the learner.

With the book completed (with the exception of the last chapter), we realized that it had actually evolved as our learning portfolio. The text represents the story of a three-year journey that two teachers took as they researched alternatives to traditional assessment. Therefore, we could best support our reading audience by following and carrying out our own advice. We needed to accompany our artifacts with a reflective narrative that would allow us to understand and extend our learning and, as a result, provide our readers with the opportunity to gain their own personal insights.

We hope that this closing reflection will reveal one of our newest discoveries about portfolios as a learning strategy: portfolios can take on new appearances with new environments. Their power is only as strong as the classroom context from which they evolved. That's why we can't "get it right"! The possibilities are endless, and our own level of understanding expands daily. That is the most exciting part for us. Unlike the traditional curriculum and tests that we used when we began our teaching careers, portfolios allow the individual learner to use them as they understand them. As the learner grows, so do the capabilities of the portfolio. Our readers have seen where we started and how we progressed. Maybe the final support will come as we share where we are as this book goes to press, and how the book supported us as we struggled with writing, implementing, and revising a new curriculum.

During the course of writing this book, our English curriculum began to take on a new appearance, creating a new environment for our portfolio usage. Starting in summer 1992, we began the process of detracking and rewriting the entire curriculum — one year at a time. As we write this final chapter, we are preparing for the summer session in which the junior curriculum will be rewritten. To begin our curriculum work, we asked for volunteers to be part of the Freshman English team. Consequently, we started our rewriting process with eight teachers (Janell was on this team) who shared a similar teaching philosophy. These were teachers who were willing to take risks and who believed wholeheartedly in the move to detrack. There was no question with this team that they wanted to replace chapter, vocabulary, and lecture-note tests with reading and writing portfolios.

Each nine weeks were guided by unit questions, and students collected artifacts they had produced in response to the short stories, poetry, artwork, novel, etc. that we read related to that question. As they assembled their portfolios, the students spread those artifacts in front of them, and then they closed their portfolio with a reflective narrative to their teacher (see Chapter 7) about the strategies they found most and least effective as they worked to improve their reading and writing. The students always closed these letters by setting the reading and writing goals that would guide them as they began the next unit. We tried to compile two portfolios for each nine-week grading period: one reading and one writing, assessing each for quality, growth, and understanding of process (see Chapter 7).

A detracked, process-focused, inquiry-based curriculum assessed with portfolios — an ideal situation. Well . . . almost! We became so involved in the reflection component of the curriculum that the portfolio was dominated by a focus on process. The metaphor of the portfolio as an autobiography of one's learning began to get lost. It became only an autobiography of one's learning process without a clear sharing of what that learner had actually learned about content along the way. The content was there; it was in every individual response the students had included within their portfolios. We were confident that their understanding of the text and their writing abilities were stronger than with our previous Freshman English curriculum. However, we weren't allowing our students to display their understanding of the question that guided the unit.

For example, Unit Two asks the students "What Are the Characteristics of Effective Literature?" Throughout their portfolios, they examine the strategies that helped them draw their conclusions regarding this question, but we never ask them to formally answer and, therefore, personalize the question. The question became lost as we struggled to cover the core curriculum and experiment with new learning strategies.

We feel confident that the strongest component of our freshman curriculum is our use of the portfolio as a learning strategy. Visitors to our classrooms are always struck by how clearly our freshmen can articulate their understanding of their own process. However, we recognize that we need to balance this process understanding with an opportunity for students to display their personal understanding of the unit question. It is an issue we will discuss with our freshmen before we close this school year as we begin our plans for the upcoming year.

Our sophomore team (of which Carol was a member) experienced almost the exact opposite problem. This team was comprised of the remainder of the teachers in our department (those who had not volunteered for the Freshman team). Therefore, initially there were issues that the Freshman team did not have to address. Several of the members of this team were not happy about the direction in which the department was headed. The one major component they did not understand was depth versus coverage, and as a compromise Carol and others with similar philosophies found themselves compromising not only what would be included as core curriculum, but also how much would be included.

Eventually a compromise was reached, in which one side conceded content coverage and the other side agreed to experiment with portfolios. As they progressed through the first unit ("How Do Cultural Beliefs Influence Lives?"), the focus at the weekly teacher curriculum meetings seemed to become "What chapter are you on?" and "When will you finish the novel?" rather than what and how are the students learning. Students moved quickly from chapter to chapter and from short story to poetry to assigned writing. In order to cover the core curriculum, learning strategies and reflection were almost completely abandoned.

At the end of the unit, Carol and her students' frustrations were heightened as they stared at the piles of "stuff" they collected in their folders throughout the unit. As the students compiled their portfolios and wrote their reflective letters, their responses were shallow and strikingly similar. They could find few artifacts that were meaningful. The portfolios were once again being used more for accountability purposes than as a learning strategy. The purpose was clearly to document coverage of core curriculum.

The portfolio's power as a vehicle to understand learners and their process was lost in a stack of activities that seemed to have very little connection and no transfer of understanding beyond the portfolio or beyond the classroom.

Carol knew something was dramatically wrong with this scenario, but she wasn't able to identify her concerns until she was invited to speak about portfolios to English teachers at our local community college. As she prepared for the presentation, she had a gnawing sense of guilt because she couldn't find any samples of student work from her current classes to support the major points she wanted to discuss. She was relying on overheads from student work that was over a year old. While talking with the teachers who attended the presentation, Carol began to see that what she believed about learning and instruction had been lost during the sophomore curriculum writing process.

She had thought that by temporarily compromising her theoretical beliefs, she could "win over" the more traditional teachers or at least pull them along in a nontraditional direction. After nearly a year of attempting to implement traditional curriculum with nontraditional methods of assessment, Carol and most of the nontraditional teachers and their students were frustrated and unmotivated. The traditional teachers were covering material as they always had and were having students assemble portfolios that resembled those accountability folders. What struck Carol, though, was that after less than two hours of sharing the stories of her previous students, most of the English teachers from the community college were enthusiastically revising their ideas about instruction and the power of reflection.

In the car on the way to our graduate class that week, we talked about her experience at the community college. What was characteristic of the times we felt frustrated and compromised? What was characteristic of those times we felt most successful, vitalized, and confident? In Carol's recent trip to the community college, she had spent an entire morning sharing student stories, and those stories had provided the basis for discussion about learning, curriculum, and instruction. The agenda for the weekly teacher's meeting within our department was also supposed to concern learning, curriculum, and instruction. However, a major component was missing between the experience Carol had at the community college and the weekly department experience: student stories. It is not compromise that will create an environment where teachers can discuss and subsequently experiment with new ideas. It is realizing the power of using student stories as the vehicles for such discussions. Our stories have been making a difference in the lives of the teachers to whom we speak at conferences and at in-service training days outside our building. We have become practiced at quickly finishing a story for each other when recalling the student and the story brings back a rush of tears. So why were we reluctant to share those same stories that had guided and inspired us with fellow teachers within our building? The very strategy that supported and fostered our growth as learners and that reassured us when we questioned if we were on the right track was students' stories about their learning.

The reading of John Mayher (1990) in our graduate class supported our use of stories. Throughout his book *Uncommon Sense*, he relates personal stories as a teacher and as a learner because "in telling each story I have been able to reflect on the experience and to change the interpretation I made at the time" (p. 99). We are surrounded daily by student stories that would allow us the same opportunity for reflection that could result in personal and professional growth.

The stories we have told throughout the book are stories about students who range from those whose parents place a high priority on ACT scores and acceptance to big name universities, to those students who are on a first name basis with the deans in our building, or work a full-time job to help pay family bills. These students continue to inspire and challenge us as teachers and learners. We want to close by encouraging you to begin immediately to listen to the stories around you, both from your students and colleagues. Encourage students to share their stories about learning with each other. But most importantly, begin to share your stories as a way to celebrate your successes and as a way to ask questions that will lead to your own personal growth as an educator and as a learner. Fill your life with those "reflective narratives that not only help the learner to understand and extend learning, but also invite the reader (listener) to gain insight about learning and the learner."

Works Cited

Anderson, Robert and John Brinnin, John Leggett, Janet Burroway, and David Leeming, eds. 1989. "Antaeus" Borden Deal. *Elements of Literature*. Third Course. Austin: Holt, Rinehart and Winston, Inc. 111–117.

_____. 1989. "The Tragedy of Romeo and Juliet." William Shakespeare. *Elements of Literature*. Third Course. Austin: Holt, Rinehart and Winston, Inc.

Babbitt, Natalie. 1975. *Tuck Everlasting*. New York: The Trumpet Club.

Bischoff, David. 1983. *War Games*. New York: Dell.

Brancato, Robin. 1977. *Winning*. New York: Alfred A. Knopf.

Calkins, Lucy. 1986. *The Art of Teaching Writing*. Portsmouth, NH: Heinemann.

Cook, Robin. 1985. *Mindbend*. New York: Berkley Books.

_____. 1988. *Mortal Fear*. New York: Berkley Books.

Crafton, Linda. 1991. *Whole Language: Getting Started Moving Forward*. New York: Richard C. Owen.

Crutcher, Chris. 1987. *The Crazy Horse Electric Game*. New York: Greenwillow.

_____. 1983. *Running Loose*. New York: Dell.

Duncan, Lois. 1989. *Don't Look Behind You*. New York: Dell.

_____. 1984. *The Third Eye*. New York: Dell.

Fulghum, Robert. 1988. *All I Really Need to Know I Learned in Kindergarten*. New York: Ivy Books.

Gilles, Carol, Mary Bixby, Paul Crowley, Shirley Crenshaw, Margaret Henrichs, Frances Reynolds, and Donelle Pyle, eds. 1988. *Whole Language Strategies for Secondary Students*. New York: Richard C. Owen.

Goodman, Yetta. 1989. "Evaluation in Whole Language Classrooms." *Teachers Networking: The Whole Language Newsletter* 4: 8–9.

Graves, Donald. 1990. International Reading Association Speech. Atlanta.

Harman, Susan. 1989–90. "The Tests: Trivial or Toxic?" *Teachers Networking The Whole Language Newsletter* 9: 1, 5–7.

Harste, Jerome, and Kathy Short, with Carolyn Burke. 1988. *Creating Classrooms for Authors: The Reading-Writing Connection*. Portsmouth, NH: Heinemann.

Hoffman, Alice. 1988. *At Risk*. New York: GP Putnam's Sons.

Jones, Ron. 1977. *The Acorn People*. New York: Bantam.

Patterson, Katherine. 1977. *Bridge to Terribithia*. New York: Avon.

Paulson, F. Leon, Pearl R. Paulson, and Carol A. Meyer. February 1991. "What Makes a Portfolio a Portfolio?" *Educational Leadership* 60–63.

The Presidential Task Force on Psychology and McREL and The American Psychological Association. 1993. "Learner-Centered Principles: Guidelines for School Redesign and Reform."

Smith, Frank. 1986. *Insult to Intelligence.* Portsmouth, NH: Heinemann.

Spielberger, Charles D. 1992. "Learner-Centered Psychological Principles: Guidelines for School Redesign and Reform." *Psychology Teacher Network.*

Steele, Danielle. 1990. *Message from Nam.* New York: Dell.

Stine, R. L. 1986. *Blind Date.* New York: Scholastic.

Thomas, John B. 1992. "The New Report Cards Portfolios Are Changing the Way Kids Get Graded." *Better Homes and Gardens* (May) 34–37.

Twain, Mark. 1988. *The Adventures of Huckleberry Finn.* New York: Bantam.

Valencia, Sheila. 1990. "A Portfolio Approach to Classroom Reading Assessment: The Whys, Whats, and Hows." *The Reading Teacher* 338-340.

Watson, Dorothy, Carolyn Burke, and Jerome Harste. 1989. *Whole Language: Inquiring Voices.* New York: Scholastic.

Watts, Sheila. 1990. *American Artist.*

White, T. H. 1965. *The Once and Future King.* New York: Berkley Publishing Group.

Wiggins, Grant. 1989. "Teaching to the (Authentic) Test." *Educational Leadership* (April) 41–46.

Williman, William. 1981. *Sunday Dinner.* Nashville: The Upper Room.

Wolf, Dennie Palmer. 1989. "Portfolio Assessment: Sampling Student Work. *Educational Leadership* (April) 35–39.

Wolfe, Denny. 1986. *Making the Grade Evaluating and Judging Student Writing.* San Diego: Coronado.

Index

writing process, reflections on, 66, 67
written conversation, 56–57, 58, 59–61
conversation, written, included in portfolios, 56–57, 58, 59–61
cookbook, as portfolio, 21–22
correctness, portfolio audience valuing, 122
counselors, as portfolio respondents, 114–115
cover of the portfolio, design considerations for the, 88
Crafton, Linda, quote on value of reflection, 35
Crazy Horse Electric Game, The, by Chris Crutcher, 6, 54
Crutcher, Chris
   Crazy Horse Electric Game, The, 6, 54
   letter to/from included in portfolio, 76, 77, 78, 81
curriculum
   experiences while detracking English, at Mundelein High School, 155–158
   portfolio examination as design strategy for the, 109
   using portfolio as learning strategy, 129–138, 139, 140–144

Darcey, play script and photographs included in portfolio, 75, 77
Dave, sample closing reflection, 98
Deeana, requesting feedback in portfolio, 104, 115
Desiree, reflecting on learning process, 37–39
detracking English at Mundelein High School, experiences while, 155–158
Diedre, reflections on writing process, 66, 67
discussions, reflections on, included in portfolio, 65
divider pages in portfolio, 90, 93, 94
Don't Look Behind You, by Lois Duncan, 17, 75
Doug, portfolio use with, 17, 18
drafts
   first through final, included in portfolio, 69, 72–73, 74
   treatment of, in traditional vs. nontraditional environments, 23, 28
Duncan, Lois
   Don't Look Behind You, 17, 75
   Third Eye, The, 21

Eryn, quotations included in portfolio, 79, 82
ethnic makeup of Mundelein High School, 3
evaluation. *See* assessment

"Evaluation in Whole Language Classrooms"
   Goodman, Yetta, 7
experimentation in learning, 45

family members, as portfolio respondents, 106, 107, 112–113, 123, 124, 125
folders, exploration of, 86
format of the portfolio, 87–88
forms
   assessment, 125, 126, 127
   conference form for responding to portfolio, 109, 111
   goal sheets, 117–118, 119
   grade sheets, use of, 131, 132, 133
   sign-in sheets for responding to portfolio, use of, 104
friends, as portfolio respondents, 106, 107, 108, 109, 110, 111, 112, 113
Fulghum, Robert, *All I Ever Needed to Know I Learned in Kindergarten,* 69

game films, as portfolios, 23, 24
Getting to Know You, 6
Glenn, in-process photographs, use of, 67, 69
goals
   conferences and, 117, 118
   goal letter sent to parents, 123, 125
   goal-setting through reflection, 48, 49
   goal sheets, 117, 118, 119
   identifying, 117, 118, 119
   instructional goal setting through portfolio examination by teacher, 109
   student reflections on achieving, 118–119
   use of sports practice tapes for setting, 138
   using portfolio as learning strategy, 129–138, 139, 140–144
Goodman, Yetta
   "Evaluation in Whole Language Classrooms," 7
   teachers as classroom researchers, 10
grades
   grade sheets, use of, 131, 132, 133
   grading portfolios, administrative requirements for, 124, 125, 126, 127
Graves, Donald, *Writing: Teachers and Children at Work,* 23
growth, validating, 48–50
Gwen
   introduction to portfolio artifact, sample, 92, 94
   "Invitation to the Reader" by, 89–90

Hemal
   risk-taking by, 44–45, 46–47

sample portfolio pages, 98–101
Hoffman, Alice, *At Risk,* 80
imaging, sketch to sketch as first step to, 58, 62
Ingrid, sample divider pages by, 94
in-process photographs included in portfolio, 66–68, 69
inquiry, celebrating, 44–47
instructional aides, as portfolio respondents, 114–115
International Reading Association, 23
"Invitation to the Reader," 89–91

Janell (teacher)
   conference form for responding to portfolio, 109, 111
   creating own portfolio, 139, 145, 146–149
   detracking freshman English curriculum, experiences during, 155–156
   development of Reading/Writing Lab. *See* Reading/Writing Lab at Mundelein High School
Jason
   mother's response to portfolio, 107
   nonfiction included in portfolio by, 73, 76
   reading journal used with, 17–20
Jim, taking responsibility for learning, 39, 41
Joe, reflecting on learning process, 37–38
Jones, Ron, *The Acorn People,* 131
Jorge, in-process photographs, use of, 67, 68
journals
   entries as portfolio items, 54–55
   sample entries
      Jason, 19–20, 34
      Mike, 55
      Rebecca, 34
      Tracey, 25–26
   walking journals, included in portfolios, 58, 62
Justin, written conversations of, 57, 59–61

Kate, in-process photographs, use of, 67, 68
Katy, in-process photographs, use of, 67, 68
Kelly
   art work included in portfolio, 75, 80
   desiring girlfriend to respond to portfolio, 106, 108
"kidwatching," 7
Kristi, portfolio construction with, 80, 83
Kuhn, use of mental imaging, 44, 45

Laura, development as enthusiastic